BE GREATER:

WHY BEING GOOD ENOUGH IS NO LONGER AN OPTION

What RIAs Do to Build Great Businesses

FIDELITY INVESTMENTS

[1]A registered investment advisor is generally defined as a person or firm that, for compensation, is engaged in the act of providing advice, making recommendations, issuing reports or furnishing analyses on securities, either directly or through publications. A registered investment advisor is registered with the Securities and Exchange Commission (SEC) or applicable state securities regulator(s).

[2]Advisors dually registered with FINRA and the SEC can do both fee- and commission-based business by leveraging platforms of their RIA (fee) and broker/dealer (commission).

[3]"RIA Marketplace 2013: The Changing Landscape of a Maturing Industry," *The Cerulli Report,* Cerulli Associates.

[4]Strategic partners are described in Chapter 1 on business models. They are firms that take a financial interest in an RIA and typically provide a range of front- and back-office services to help the RIA run its business.

[5]These stories are provided by clients of Fidelity Institutional Wealth Services (IWS), a business unit within Fidelity Brokerage Services LLC that provides custody and brokerage services to intermediaries. Their business needs and experiences may not reflect the experience of other IWS clients or all RIAs.

200 Seaport Boulevard, Boston, MA 02210

ISBN 978-0-9906624-0-2
682269.1.0 1.9860459.100

"If history were taught in the form of stories, it would neve be forgotten." RUDYARD KIPLING

Moving the Dial—Making a Financial Advisory Firm Greater

Registered investment advisors (RIAs)[1] have certainly been performing well when it comes to accumulating assets. In fact, Cerulli Associates is predicting that independent and dually registered[2] firms will account for 26% of all retail advisory assets by the end of 2016.[3] As this growth accelerates, so, too, does competition, making it more challenging for firms to stand apart from others and attract the best clients and the best associates. This means being good enough is no longer an option—you have to strive to be greater to continue to be a destination of choice for discerning investors and talented professionals.

So, what are RIAs doing to move their businesses forward? They are consolidating and adding to their bench strength and geographic coverage, evaluating different growth tracks and aligning with strategic partners[4] that bring money and expertise to the table, and accessing better and more customized solutions to drive additional efficiencies and productivity. In short, they are positioning themselves as a force to be reckoned with.

We are often asked what others in the field are doing, and what insights can be drawn from their experiences. This book shares the stories of more than 20 advisors who have been taking thoughtful steps—and calculated risks—to move the dial.[5] Before we introduce their firms, let's take a brief look at how RIAs got to where they are today, and discuss five areas we feel are important for firms to concentrate on if they are to continue to flourish.

SOME HISTORY

Many things have contributed to the high rate of growth we are witnessing. A major factor was the impact of the financial meltdown of 2008 that drove a large number of wirehouse advisors to consider the independent route. "After the market crash, I think the world viewed Wall Street a little more cynically and saw independent RIAs as the white knight," says Blaine Lourd, Managing Member of LourdMurray. "Small RIAs could easily get an audience with high-net-worth individuals. Guys like me from the sell side started firms with the simple idea of providing conflict-free advice that put the client's interests first, and best-of-breed solutions that addressed their problems."

As more RIAs were established, enterprising third parties saw opportunities to support an expanding channel. These included strategic partners that introduced new models to facilitate the formation of highly sophisticated independent advisory firms. "We took advantage of this and went independent in 2010 with the help of a strategic partner," says Greg Erwin, Co-Founder and Partner of Sapient Private Wealth Management. "It provided the money and know-how to help make our transition a success, while enabling us to retain our brand and independence. It's far more doable today than at any time in the past for large advisory teams to easily make the move to independence—and they are doing it."

Of course, this growth was also driven by the need to introduce new capabilities to meet changing investor demands. We saw firms form family offices to serve their ultra-high-net-worth clients, add asset management solutions to provide additional investment choices, and introduce retirement services to support clients who were business owners and had benefit plans for their employees. Today, we are seeing RIAs further expand their offerings to support the emerging wealthy, and leveraging technology to provide cost-efficient planning and advice services to the mass-affluent market.

CHANGE CONTINUES

While it may sound like an overused phrase to say the world is moving at an incredibly fast pace, this is definitely true in the RIA space. Competitors have become partners, and alliances and acquisitions have enabled an entirely different type of firm to take shape. Of course, technology is having a dramatic impact on the business as well. On the mobile front alone, increased Internet speeds and slick smartphones and tablets are redefining client interactions and the way in which many financial consultations and presentations are handled. Even the type of investor being served is changing, as thousands of baby boomers turn 65 every day and wealth continues to transfer between generations and genders.

> "If RIAs want dynamic growth, they have to continually adjust their businesses to keep up." MARTY BICKNELL, CEO MARINER HOLDINGS

"With all that's going on, it's imperative to continually evaluate your RIA business," explains Marty Bicknell, CEO of Mariner Holdings. "The model has to adjust on a consistent basis if you are to stay cutting edge." Bicknell's firm is an example of this type of evolution. In 2006, he left a regional broker-dealer to form a small RIA. Since then, the company has been growing both organically and through acquisitions. Today, he runs Mariner Holdings, a 35+ billion dollar operation that focuses on wealth and asset management through subsidiaries Mariner Wealth Advisors and Montage Investments. In 2013, Bicknell also took steps to further expand his business by entering the mass market with FirstPoint Financial, a firm that provides a unique financial planning offering to investors of all asset sizes.

In part, this book discusses some of these changes that have become a reality for independent financial advisory firms. Primarily, though, it looks at how you can capitalize on market developments to help propel your own organization to the next level—whether you are a large firm or a small one.

Five Points of View

Over the years, we have engaged in hundreds of outreach activities with our clients. Many of these have involved helping them evaluate their business to identify areas of strength and opportunities for improvement. Our work has been supported by a series of benchmarking studies we have conducted, along with in-depth advisor and investor surveys. In addition, we have developed numerous thought-leadership pieces that have delved into the traits of firms that perform well. As this work has progressed, we have formed five points of view on what we believe it takes to be a robust RIA that's in tune with investor and competitor dynamics. Our points of view center on (1) business models, (2) planning, (3) technology, (4) client engagement, and (5) teams.

To provide more depth and to better illustrate these five points of view, we decided to interview a number of our clients to create a compilation of stories that show what they have done in each of these areas. We felt stories could educate and engage other advisors, provide concrete examples to bring things to life, and help make any issues that may be somewhat complex a little easier to understand.

We also decided to complement these stories with practical steps and considerations to serve as an actionable guide for change. Thus, we combine these real-life experiences with some textbook theory that's captured in sections throughout the book titled "Connecting the Dots." We hope this will provide a number of "aha" moments for you that can have a positive impact on your activities—whether you are an RIA today or just considering this option for independence.

CHAPTERS OF THE BOOK ARE ORGANIZED AROUND OUR FIVE POINTS OF VIEW:

Business Models: Evolving business models present new opportunities.

Many different operating models exist today for how independent financial advisors can structure their business, and new versions continue to emerge to enhance efficiencies, client service, and profitability. You can run things on your own, outsource different functions to a third party, affiliate with a partner for financial and operational support, grow through acquisitions, and more. By keeping a close eye on what's feasible—and appropriate—for a business at different points in its life cycle, firms striving to be greater have avoided stagnation and honed their structure to take advantage of new developments and new offerings.

One example is The Colony Group, a longtime RIA that affiliated with a strategic partner in 2011 to gain the support and resources needed to move to the next stage of its development. "We were thinking big and looking to grow," recounts Michael Nathanson, Chairman, CEO, and President. "We saw an opportunity to make that happen by taking advantage of a new strategic model." The partner provided capital for Colony to make three significant acquisitions, enabling the 28-year-old firm to triple its assets under management (AUM) in under three years. We discuss Colony and a range of other business model stories in Chapter 1.

Planning: Planning creates focus to drive success.

In an environment where readiness matters, being reactive no longer feels like a feasible option. Having a well-defined roadmap and a strong commitment to seeing activities through is critical to meeting longer-term goals. Firms need to see prioritization and planning as integral to running a successful business, whether it's a strategic plan that lays out a vision for a firm and clear action steps to get there, or a succession plan that describes what will happen when a partner decides to retire.

Buckingham Asset Management is an example of a firm that values the power of planning. "While we had strategic and marketing plans in place," says CEO Adam Birenbaum, "we knew we also needed to plot out the next chapter in our history. This required a succession plan to ensure that the upcoming generation of leaders would have the skills and experience to continue the legacy that had been built. We created an internal leadership path that would grow the next crop of individuals who could take over management." We discuss Buckingham and other strategic and succession planning stories in Chapter 2.

Technology: Harnessing technology enhances the client experience. Getting a firm's technology infrastructure right and using capabilities to their fullest are obviously critical in an industry that's heavily reliant on systems for trading, reporting, compliance, client communications, and more. We found that firms striving to be greater have a well-rounded view of technology: They align their technology strategy with their business strategy, and see it working in tandem with their processes and their people. They also take the time to keep technology up to date, eliminate redundancies, and streamline operations as much as possible. This often includes auditing what's currently in place and introducing capabilities that leverage advances in the marketplace, such as cloud computing and mobile applications. They do this while always ensuring that new initiatives fit with the firm's overall direction, and aren't simply distracting—albeit enjoyable—fads.

Halbert Hargrove Global Advisors has long understood the importance of technology and the positive impact it can have on both the client and employee experience—if done well. "Integration among applications has always been a priority for us to make workflows as seamless as possible, and many processes are run through one system," says Russ Hill, Chairman and CEO. In Chapter 3, we discuss Halbert Hargrove and other technology stories.

Client Engagement: Attracting and retaining the right clients propels business forward.

As we have said, while the RIA segment has flourished, competition has also intensified, making it more difficult for advisors to stand out from the pack. Companies need to reevaluate who they serve today and who they may want to serve tomorrow, tighten up their value proposition and firm story, and look at new engagement models to stay relevant and in demand.

The team at Sand Hill Global Advisors took a close look at the firm's strengths and what that meant for the type of client they could best serve. "We used these insights to create a number of specialty areas that would enable us to concentrate on select investor groups, helping us develop known areas of expertise to support our business development activities," says Jane Williams, Chair and Co-Founder. Chapter 4 describes Sand Hill's efforts and provides other stories about attracting and retaining the right type of client.

Teams: Hiring and developing top talent supports growth.

The final area, although not last in importance in any way, is the recognition that the individuals who clients work with make a big difference, and that happy and highly motivated staff members are essential for an exceptional client experience. Firms striving to be greater know that strong teams can be a win all around, so they take steps to build and maintain a collaborative and rewarding environment. The process begins with the contact made in a prospective employee's initial interview, and carries through to how well that employee's performance evaluations are handled once he or she is on board.

RMB Capital looks to recruit based not only on the right skill set, but also on alignment with the firm's vision and values. This congruity fosters a collaborative culture of people who are united behind the common goal of serving clients' best interests. "A strong focus on training and development, including clear career paths, regular reviews, and a mentorship model, helps to keep employees challenged and motivated," says Richard Burridge, Founding Partner, CEO, and Chief Investment Officer. Chapter 5 delves deeper into RMB and other stories about talent development strategies.

If your firm is to perform well, vacillating isn't an option—you have to address these five areas head on, and recognize that they need to work together if you are going to be firing on all cylinders. After all, it's hard to know which business model is best if you don't have a long-term vision for the firm; the type of people you need if you haven't thought about your growth strategy; and the technology that may be required if you haven't clearly defined your target market. While this may sound daunting, by bringing together real-life stories, with practical steps and considerations on how to move forward, we hope we can help make the journey an easier one.

OTHER RESOURCES TO BE GREATER

This book works in conjunction with begreater.com, which is referenced in the Connecting the Dots sections. Visit the site to read articles and white papers and watch videos that provide additional ideas and considerations about the topics covered in each chapter.

[1]

Evolving Business Models Present New Opportunities

2 OR 3

The number of different business models advisors look at before going independent*

*The Fidelity Insights on Independence study was conducted by an independent third-party research firm not affiliated with Fidelity Investments between September 26 and October 13, 2011, among 173 advisors who had moved to an independent model. These advisors had made the move within the past five years and had a minimum book of business of $10 million in assets under management. Fidelity Investments wasn't revealed as the sponsor.

Models

> "When you're finished changing, you're finished." BENJAMIN FRANKLIN

There are many different operating models for RIAs today, and new ones are continually emerging to better serve the needs of clients and help owners realize their longer-term vision. We see firms taking stock of the myriad choices that are available for going independent, and for expanding and changing current structures to stay competitive. In this chapter, we look at three trends we are observing as RIAs try to accelerate their businesses. They are trying to (1) find the best structure that fits the objectives and culture of the firm, (2) shore up bench strength through mergers and acquisitions (M&A), and (3) diversify to strengthen the balance sheet and reach new markets.

Find the Best Structure

Learn About

- Advisory teams that have established their own RIAs
- Handing off functions to outside experts
- Different types of strategic partners and their support models

As advisors go independent to achieve a certain level of autonomy and control, there are various ways to structure the business. Some choose to establish their own firm and handle all the managerial and operational aspects, while others choose to partner with a third party for assistance. Whatever route is taken, it's clear that business models have become much more dynamic—what works today may not be ideal for tomorrow. From the stories we have heard, RIAs are willing to make changes to suit their needs. These include traditional RIAs shifting their models to align with third parties to drive growth.

Two major third-party options include functional outsourcers and strategic partners. Functional outsourcers may specialize in investment, compliance, human resources (HR), or other service offerings. Over the past several years, we have also seen the emergence of larger organizations that provide comprehensive, end-to-end capabilities, including extensive technology platforms and research.

Strategic partners may invest in or purchase advisory firms and provide a host of services to help grow the business. They come in many different flavors, including an affiliate and employee model, each with distinct philosophies, structures, and

"Newer business models are repositioning the independent space for the next leg of growth."

ALAN HARTER, MANAGING DIRECTOR
PACTOLUS PRIVATE WEALTH MANAGEMENT

modes of operation. In the affiliate model, the strategic partner is a facilitator and investor, typically working with larger entrepreneurial RIAs who want assistance with executing a growth strategy, while retaining their brand, culture, and autonomy. These strategic partners may provide assistance with planning and marketing, and bring leads and capital to the table for business transactions.

In the employee model, advisors typically take on the brand of the strategic partner and have access to a range of services and in-house expertise. Based on comments from our interviewees, there are a number of approaches for this model. For example, advisors may choose to give a percentage of their cash flow to the strategic partner without receiving equity, sell part of their firm in exchange for equity, or join as partners and share in the overall revenues of the firm.

To provide insights into some of the options that are available, we share stories about advisors who chose to form an RIA and run things on their own or with the help of outsourcers, and others who chose to leverage a strategic partner model.

FORM AN RIA AND RUN THINGS ON YOUR OWN OR WITH THE HELP OF OUTSOURCERS

DISCOVER COMPLETE INDEPENDENCE

John Waldron, Founder and CEO of Waldron Wealth Management, has been in business serving ultra-high-net-worth clients since 1995. Over time, his firm has taken some dramatic steps to adjust its service model and gain additional independence.

SAYS WALDRON:

When we talk about what it takes to be great in the advisory space, I would say you always have to be introspective and challenge what's not broken to keep on the cutting edge. We certainly are no stranger to change.

When the firm was formed in 1995, we decided to affiliate with an independent broker-dealer. The business was doing well, but it was clear it could be even better if clients were segmented and were offered specific professional support to meet their unique needs. About ten years ago, we took a major step and split the company into two divisions: private wealth management that focuses on corporate executives and professionals with high earnings, and a multifamily office that focuses on business owners and inheritors of wealth. This enables us to provide a continuum of services as a client's financial picture changes.

"We saw the move to our own RIA as a chance to be more independent and to partner with people who understand the ultra-high-net-worth space." JOHN WALDRON

We took another major step forward in 2012. Clients were looking for access to a broader range of capabilities and we felt we needed to become completely independent to offer new services. Because there are many ways to do this, we considered a lot of different alternatives, from establishing our own RIA to joining another firm to affiliating with a strategic partner. In the end, we set up our own RIA.

We then thought about who we wanted to partner with for custodial services, technology, and research, and we sent out formal requests for proposals. After about four to six weeks evaluating and scoring the contenders, we made our decisions. From there, we put detailed project timelines in place to keep the transition on track.

In order to make a major strategic decision like this work, you need a culture that accepts change and is willing to implement it on behalf of the company. It was clear we could deliver a better client experience this way, and our staff was fully behind the move.

We also took the opportunity to trim our client roster during the transition. Over time, you take on some relationships as a courtesy. We looked at who was in our sweet spot where we could provide the most value. Where there wasn't a strong fit, we introduced clients to other advisors we felt were more appropriate, making it a win all around. Sharpening the definition of who we are, what we want to be, and the type of client we are best suited for was a critical exercise as we started the next leg of our history. [You'll hear more about identifying ideal clients in Chapter 4 on client engagement.]

Key Insight

Different factors drive firms to become an RIA, and there are many ways to approach this today. Take the time to evaluate the benefits of various business models to determine which one is the best for you and your team.

BECOME AN ENTREPRENEUR — WITH ASSISTANCE

In 2006, Blaine Lourd, Managing Member of LourdMurray, decided to become independent. He established an RIA and outsourced a number of functions to concentrate on serving his clients. Over time, he brought in additional management talent and new advisors to continue to grow the firm.

SAYS LOURD:

I had been in the business about twenty years and had moved around a bit searching for the panacea on the sell side. I knew it was time to make the leap to independence and pursue the American Dream of entrepreneurship. So I worked with a custodian to understand all the things I needed to have in place to run my own RIA — from the operational side to selecting a designer for my office space. Then I hired a lawyer, set up an LLC, and was ready to go. I think a lot of people overthink the start-up phase. Quite honestly, it's not that difficult and you can be up and running in a few months' time if you work hard at it.

> "In the end, going independent is the best thing I ever did from a self-actualization, business, and income point of view." BLAINE LOURD

While we wanted to handle many aspects of the business ourselves, we chose to outsource a number of functions, including payroll, HR, and compliance, to specialists in these areas. We needed to do what we do best, which is managing clients and gathering assets.

Since then, I have been adding resources and expanding the business, including bringing on a new president. Palmer Murray and I had been longtime friends. He had been working at a wirehouse and admired the fact that I had taken this entrepreneurial risk and built an RIA, so we discussed having him join the firm. It took us four years to consummate the partnership, but it was worth it.

We continue to look for like-minded individuals who believe in our approach to investing and financial planning and, of course, who fit our culture. We added an advisor in New Orleans, my home town, and are planning to ramp up our expansion strategy this year. While we are looking at locations where there are synergies with our business, in the end it's all about the people. If they can add value, we'll find a way to open an office wherever they are located. [You'll hear more about LourdMurray's strategies for attracting and retaining top talent in Chapter 5 on building strong teams.]

Key Insight

It's essential for any new firm to quickly get on a growth path. Although you may choose to run most aspects of the business yourself, consider outsourcing functions that aren't your areas of expertise so you can spend more time with prospects and clients.

GAIN IMMEDIATE SCALE

Alan Harter, Managing Director of Pactolus Private Wealth Management, affiliated with a functional outsourcer to put his new RIA into motion by leveraging existing capabilities. This helped to scale the business and obtain advantageous pricing, given the partner's size and buying power.

SAYS HARTER:

There was a push to go independent because my clients were becoming disenchanted with the larger investment bank model after reading negative comments about their advisory firm in the press. There was also a pull because I knew I could implement a broader spectrum of solutions as an RIA.

> "I knew I needed to go independent if I were to continue to grow my business with families who require sophisticated and highly customized services." ALAN HARTER

I realized I could get instant scale by working with Dynasty Financial Partners, a large functional outsourcer that helps advisors gain access to investment products, research from a wide selection of providers, and comprehensive technology resources for the front and back office.

When you look at a smaller firm like ours, the only way you can accelerate critical mass and meet client needs is to have a relationship with a quality third party. Firms like Dynasty are taking steps to really differentiate advisors who use their platform by leveraging their scale to provide resources others may not be able to afford on their own.

Today we are seeing institutional investors come into the market backing functional outsourcers financially. This influx of money will enable additional growth to occur as this model continues to gain traction. With all these changes, without a doubt, good is no longer good enough. If you aren't continually trying to evolve your business and offer greater services, transparency, and opportunity, you run the risk of becoming irrelevant.

Key Insight

Access to robust capabilities is key to getting a new RIA up and running in a short period of time. You may want to work with a functional outsourcer that can provide immediate access to high-quality infrastructure that can help you scale—and differentiate—your business.

AFFILIATE WITH A STRATEGIC PARTNER

FOCUS ON CORE COMPETENCIES

Although Bob DiQuollo, CEO and Principal of Brinton Eaton Wealth Advisors, had been operating as an RIA for many years, he chose to affiliate with a strategic partner that provided the opportunity to be part of a network of advisors and hand off time-consuming, non-core tasks to experts.

SAYS DIQUOLLO:

We founded Brinton Eaton twenty-five years ago. We had a nice business and were doing great work for our clients, but felt we were getting too involved with compliance issues, HR, payroll, and back-office activities. I would say we were betwixt and between—big enough that we needed all these things, but too small to want to invest a lot of money and time in them. We knew we needed a partner if we were going to get to the next level, so we joined forces with Marty Bicknell's firm, Mariner Wealth Advisors.

We looked at about five different models before making a move, including joining a bank and merging with another firm. In the end, we did a deal that let us add more arrows to our quiver while staying independent. We retain our name and manage our own clients, but now we have this superstructure behind us. Mariner has specialists on board in a range of functions who can provide high-quality support, including marketing, accounting, HR—you name it. Whenever we need help, I know there is someone I can call who spends one-hundred percent of their time in that area. We can also share ideas with other advisory firms that are part of the Mariner family.

"We wanted a partner that could free us up to spend more time on client-facing activities. It's made life much easier, and has made us so much more efficient." BOB DIQUOLLO

I think a firm that performs well is one that can handle a large volume of business while providing great service to clients. This deal takes away many administrative tasks that consume a lot of time so we can concentrate on important client issues. It has also given us long-term security by providing funds for the younger people in the firm to buy out the older ones. Our staff and clients can now be confident that we'll remain here with independent ownership and a strong partner as an investor.

Key Insight

You can affiliate with a strategic partner to gain access to extensive resources and financing while retaining your independence. This may be a route to pursue if you are looking to extend the capabilities of your firm without adding more staff.

TAP INTO EXPERTISE

When Greg Erwin, Co-Founder and Partner of Sapient Private Wealth Management, and his colleagues went independent, they leveraged the experience and know-how of a strategic partner that assisted with a lot of early-stage decision making. This helped the firm quickly gain traction and avoid costly mistakes.

SAYS ERWIN:

After being lifelong employees of a wirehouse, we began to see a cultural change and knew we had to move on. We looked at a number of different options, but we were new to the independent space and didn't know that much about it. As a result, we weren't comfortable taking a sizable business and trying to do something on our own, so we chose to affiliate with Focus Financial Partners.

We received excellent assistance as we set up our business, which included a practical view about what we should be considering given the type of firm we were building and our stage of development. Our strategic partner presented different solutions and discussed pricing and implementation issues. It saved us a lot of time narrowing down the choices.

"Without the expertise of this partner, we would have been so far behind where we are today. They let us hit the ground running." GREG ERWIN

They also provided capital and expertise to address several other issues, including an internal restructuring of ownership. Today, I can proudly say we are a high-end, national wealth management firm that's growing and that has a stable and scalable platform.

Key Insight

A lack of familiarity with the independent space can be a concern for advisors who are thinking about establishing an RIA. Consider working with a partner that knows the ins and outs of the business and can help you with critical decision making as you set up your firm.

CAPITALIZE ON BUSINESS GROWTH

Kelly Trevethan, Regional Managing Director of United Capital Financial Advisers, was looking for the freedom and flexibility to be a true entrepreneur, so he and his team joined a strategic partner that has an employee model.

SAYS TREVETHAN:

After the credit crisis of 2008, there were lots of forced marriages taking place with big financial institutions. I didn't like what I was seeing, so I decided to join United Capital Financial Advisers. Joe Duran, CEO and founder of the firm, had been a client of mine. After he sold his company back in 2001, I said if he created an independent organization that was national in scope, fully transparent, and offered best-of-breed solutions, he could attract top talent. He started United Capital in 2004 and my team moved over in 2008.

"I went independent to have the opportunity to continue to grow my business, control how I ran things, and be compensated as an entrepreneur." KELLY TREVETHAN

Under this model, advisors join United Capital as employees and take on the firm's name and branding, which covers about fifty offices across the country. The firm represents a place where someone can plug in and benefit from the extensive services being provided, which include innovative tools that have been developed for working with clients. Advisors also benefit from the exceptional national media exposure that Joe receives.

Advisors come on board and continue to manage their book of business as they did previously, while tapping into all these resources. They can also sell their future revenue stream in exchange for stock in the company. Equity was important for me, so I said, "Make me a shareholder." You want to have a stake in an organization you believe in and that's growing so you can have a significant wealth event down the road.

Key Insight

Having equity ownership may be a requirement for you so you have more invested in the success of the firm. If so, find a partner that provides an opportunity to benefit financially from its long-term growth.

JOIN A PARTNERSHIP

Jordan Waxman, Managing Director and Partner of HSW Advisors, HighTower, and his colleagues were looking to go independent. They considered a number of different models before settling on a solution that would enable them to act as partners with other respected advisory teams.

SAYS WAXMAN:

As we looked at the RIA channel, we had to decide whether we would go fully independent and run our own firm or join an established organization that already had accomplished much of the groundbreaking work. We elected the latter. We looked at several models and consulted with friends who were fully independent before making our decision in 2012 to join HighTower, a strategic partner.

We saw that HighTower had traction, and had brought on a number of very good advisory teams. We were impressed with their infrastructure and management, and thought they had a sound strategy for growth. We are very happy that we came on board, especially as the company continues to mature.

> "We chose to go independent to enable us to source robust solutions and act solely in the best interests of our clients." JORDAN WAXMAN

There are three different ways to be part of HighTower: partnership, network, and alliance models. We joined in the partnership model, which creates a very different environment. All the teams like HSW Advisors are looking to share ideas and best practices for the common good of the firm. The aim is on having the pie grow, and everyone pitches in to make that happen.

All the partners have a large voice in setting priorities for the company. We participate on advisory councils and on HighTower's Board of Directors, so we are helping to set the course for the firm. Teams in the partnership also use the HighTower brand to some degree, which helps with market impact.

Key Insight

Interacting with other advisory teams can help identify new ideas and best practices. Many strategic partnership models provide the opportunity to connect with other like-minded advisors who are part of the network.

[1.1]

CONNECTING THE DOTS

EVOLVE YOUR BUSINESS MODEL

Set Up an RIA

The stories RIAs have shared show that there are many different ways to set up and operate an RIA today depending on your size, service model, and growth strategy. You can do it alone or work with functional outsourcers or strategic partners that provide a spectrum of alternatives for tapping into proven platforms.

A number of differences exist within and across these alternatives, so look closely at each one to understand their nuances and the implications for access to services, financial support, independence, and client ownership.

Work with Functional Outsourcers or Strategic Partners

If functional outsourcers or strategic partners are on your radar screen, consider taking the following steps to help you zero in on the business model that's best for you and your team:

- Outline your long-term vision and how you plan to grow the business.
- List what you are looking for in a relationship, such as back-office support, money for business transactions, a succession strategy, and/or the ability to work with like-minded advisors.
- Do your due diligence so you understand the models that are available, and the pros and cons of each.
- Be realistic about your personality, need for control, and desire to work with others.
- Assess your own, and your firm's, strengths and weaknesses.
- Ask yourself if you want to manage all the business, or maintain control without day-to-day responsibility for functions like investment management, administration, and back-office issues. Keep in mind that you'll still need to pay attention to these activities and monitor them, even if you turn them over to a functional outsourcer or strategic partner to handle.
- Determine if you are willing to sell part of your firm in return for financial support.

 **Go to begreater.com to access additional resources supporting Chapter 1.**

Shore Up Bench Strength with Mergers and Acquisitions

Learn About

- Clearly defining the attributes of an ideal target firm
- Taking time to test the cultural fit
- Getting clients and staff on board with a change
- Understanding the potential challenges with implementation

Many people believe there are a number of industry trends under way that will accelerate the consolidation we are seeing in the RIA space. Adam Birenbaum, CEO of Buckingham Asset Management and BAM Advisor Services, is one of these individuals.

"First of all, investors are looking to work with comprehensive wealth managers, so firms will need to expand their service offering," he says. "Then there's the turnover that's happening among older advisors. This will provide an opportunity for larger RIAs to offer a succession solution and emerge as a destination for advisors and their clients."

To create this scale, RIAs are merging with or acquiring other firms. Some are looking to share costs and create critical mass. Others want to bring together different skill sets and market niches, or put in place a transition strategy to smoothly exit the business down the road. The firms interviewed for this book touted the benefits of these types of transactions, but they also said they aren't

> "M&A will provide RIAs the size and scale to compete with the largest financial services organizations."
>
> ADAM BIRENBAUM, CEO
> BUCKINGHAM ASSET MANAGEMENT AND BAM ADVISOR SERVICES

for everyone. Deals can take a lot of time and effort, and you need to be well prepared to handle integration issues after they are complete. Given this, you should have a clear understanding of why it makes sense to proceed with a transaction before moving forward. The stories that follow describe the M&A strategies of three RIAs.

ADD TALENT AND GEOGRAPHIC COVERAGE

Adam Birenbaum led Buckingham Asset Management in completing six transactions between 2010 and 2013, strengthening the firm's lineup of thought leaders, and expanding representation in numerous cities.

SAYS BIRENBAUM:

We did our first transaction in 2010 when we combined forces with Wealth Management Consultants (WMC), whose founder had been a colleague and longtime friend of our team. Then in 2011, we merged with RNM Financial Management. We got to know the founder through our sister firm BAM Advisor Services, which had been providing back-office services to RNM since 1999. Our similar approach to wealth management made the decision to merge a simple one.

"You always do M&A with the idea that one plus one equals three. We have added tremendous resources and new offices as a result." ADAM BIRENBAUM

Later in 2011, KB Investment Advisors joined our ranks. Like RNM, their philosophy dovetailed perfectly with ours. In 2012, we added Prasada Capital Management, whose founder became our director of investor education, strengthening our lineup of educators. Our next merger was with Founders Financial Network in California, which enhanced our ability to serve the Silicon Valley market. In 2013, we expanded down south through a deal with JWA Financial Group, whose founder also added to our thought leadership capabilities since he was a host of an economic and investment radio show. [You'll hear how Buckingham is using thought leadership to enhance market visibility in Chapter 4 on client engagement.]

We look at a set of criteria before getting into the economics of a deal:

- First is culture—we want to make sure these are individuals who think and act like we do.
- Second is investment ideology—we believe in passive investing, and are interested in firms that share this ideology.
- Third is the client service experience—we want firms that follow an integrated, comprehensive wealth management approach, and that truly believe that by coming together we can be even better.

Once we have addressed these three issues, the economics need to make sense. From there, it's about integration and, ultimately, super-charging the business.

Key Insight

M&A isn't just about growth—it's about smart growth. Thoughtfully look at what each potential merger or acquisition can add to the capabilities and market coverage of the overall enterprise before moving forward with any deal.

BETTER SERVE STAKEHOLDERS

Michael Nathanson, Chairman, CEO, and President of The Colony Group, sees M&A as an opportunity to combine forces with other fiduciary advisors* to better serve the firm's clients, employees, and partners.

SAYS NATHANSON:

The Colony Group was founded in March 1986, making us one of the oldest independent, fee-only wealth managers in New England. While we were already a large firm in 2011, we wanted to accelerate growth and felt the right transaction would let us combine resources, have a deeper and broader team, and a more comprehensive offering for our clients. In addition, we felt it would position us to attract, develop, and retain the best people in the industry—and, as a service industry, it's all about having the best people. If you don't continue to grow, it's difficult to demonstrate a clear path toward professional and economic fulfillment.

*Fiduciaries are hired to act in a client's best interest and must set aside any personal motives to pursue the best outcome for a client's particular situation.

I believe a number of things need to be in place for a deal to work, including:

- Good infrastructure to be able to scale the business
- People who are dedicated to integration and support in order to ensure that the transaction doesn't interfere with serving clients
- Credibility and deal expertise, because there is no such thing as a simple merger or acquisition, regardless of size
- Capital, which can be much more difficult to raise than people often think

"We felt we were a great firm on our own, but could fundamentally be better if we came together with another great firm." MICHAEL NATHANSON

Although we had the infrastructure in place, we felt we needed a partner for the expertise, experience, and funds. We joined forces with Focus Financial Partners in 2011, and have been able to close three deals since.

Mintz Levin Financial Advisors was the first transaction, a sizable firm in its own right at the time. This was followed in 2013 by a smaller deal with Prosper Advisors, which expanded our footprint into New York. In 2014, we acquired Long Wharf Investors in Boston.

We are a highly disciplined organization and developed acquisition guidelines to identify the right type of candidates. In addition to certain financial metrics, we want fee-only advisors who have a fiduciary model, a compatible investment philosophy, a high client retention rate, and a relatively low client-to-advisor ratio. Naturally, we are also looking to acquire good talent, so qualifications, tenure, and integrity come into play as well.

People are rightly concerned about cultural fit, too. I think firms that have a fiduciary model and are fee-only have a client-centric approach, which helps make the culture similar. The key point is not to rush—you need to take your time and really get to know one another, and feel these are people you would like to work with.

There are a number of additional issues to take into account when considering inorganic growth. Change is uncomfortable for people, so you have to try hard not to be threatening to the other party. It's also important that employees understand the value proposition for them, so continuous communication is essential. Of course, you need to be super sensitive to client needs, and show this has been a good move that will provide them with substantial benefits.

With Mintz Levin Financial Advisors, for example, we communicated extensively with both sets of clients—ours and theirs. As a joint team, we outlined all the reasons we wanted to do this and how clients would benefit. We sent letters and followed up with phone calls to make sure we were able to answer any and all questions.

Key Insight

The right culture can make or break a deal, so spend enough time on the "getting to know you" stage. In addition, you can't afford to lose employee or client trust during a period of change, so communicate regularly with stakeholders and explain what's happening and how they'll benefit.

PLAN FOR A SUCCESSFUL INTEGRATION

Bob Glovsky, Vice Chair and Senior Financial Counselor of The Colony Group and former President of Mintz Levin Financial Advisors, says you need to think carefully about integration as firms merge, and map out a detailed plan of action.

SAYS GLOVSKY:

Even before we closed the deal, we listed the ten areas of integration we thought we had to tackle, and what the challenges would likely be.

"While integration can be difficult, with the right attitude you can come up with a better product and a better company." BOB GLOVSKY

Some areas were easy to handle, like employee benefits, compensation, and office space. The three we thought would take time involved integrating our investment offerings, creating a common approach to the delivery of financial planning, and aligning the back office. By having people from both firms work closely together, we have made great progress on all three and have been able to identify and implement best practices.

Although Colony will continue to look for new opportunities, we have to be measured about any kind of merger or acquisition opportunity. Growing too fast in an unmoderated fashion could present other risks. We want to protect our culture, which is one more commonly found in smaller companies, and we want to adhere to the principles of excellence in client service.

Key Insight

Integration after a deal is completed can be a challenge. Be realistic about what you'll need to do and the areas that will likely be most difficult, and create a game plan that involves people from both firms.

BUILD OUT SPECIFIC COMPETENCIES

Peter Raimondi, Founder and CEO of Banyan Partners, saw the opportunity to create an RIA that provided customized portfolios for high-net-worth investors using in-house resources. He acquired a firm that could serve as a platform for his vision, then further built the infrastructure.

SAYS RAIMONDI:

Banyan is the second firm I have started, and my vision was to create an RIA that offered custom asset management services, building portfolios with in-house resources. A custom shop requires a lot of talent. Because people are your most expensive asset, you sacrifice some of your margin as a result. Nonetheless, I felt there was an opportunity here and that we could be successful.

In 2008, I spent a lot of time trying to identify a firm that I could buy and build out as the platform for what I wanted to do. I was looking for an RIA that did individual equity management, had a good team, and was excited about my vision. I found that firm in Oaktree Asset Management in New York, headed by David Bottoms. David had a staff of eight people that included two portfolio managers and a compliance officer. It was important for me that the leader stay involved in the business, and David remains an equity holder in Banyan, sits on our Board, and is an active portfolio manager.

Our growth strategy has always been multifaceted: We have grown organically and have closed seven transactions in five years. Our external expansion started in 2011 when we accidentally came across two interesting opportunities. One was a three-person operation in Boston, and the other a division of Weiss Research, a firm that produces newsletters. We suspected that there would be a lot of client attrition with the Weiss deal because it wasn't a high-touch business, but the firm had very talented people, including four portfolio managers, two client advisors, and an in-house marketing department. Sherri Daniels, our chief operating officer today, came from this organization.

We then acquired another small firm whose owner was looking for a succession strategy, and by 2013 we felt we had a great roster of portfolio managers and research analysts, and geographic presence up the East Coast. Good press coverage resulted in a string of very interesting candidates, and we ended up "getting married" three times that year. This included the large acquisition of Silver Bridge Advisors in Boston, a firm twice our size in terms of AUM. Silver Bridge had many suitors, but chose us because they wanted to be a part of what we were building. The firm enabled us to broaden our wealth management capabilities while expanding our footprint with its multifamily office in San Francisco.

"I wanted to create something unique in our space, and grow it into a sizable business." PETER RAIMONDI

We further rounded out our capabilities with the acquisition of Texas-based Rushmore Investment Advisors, which brought us institutional assets and a very articulate international portfolio. The next deal was with Wisconsin-based Holt-Smith Advisors, a firm that was adept at stock picking and building custom portfolios.

My advice to firms considering acquisitions is to have the infrastructure and people in place first — it's a big mistake to acquire a firm and not be prepared for the transition. On another note, I think it's important to give equity in the firm to other people, so they can share in the growth and be part of the excitement.

Key Insight

Acquisitions should complement the overall strategic direction of the firm. By understanding the type of firm you are today—and want to be tomorrow—you can take a good look at opportunities you come across to determine whether they are appropriate to pursue.

BE AWARE OF THE "SOFTER" ISSUES

Sherri Daniels, Chief Operating Officer of Banyan Partners, emphasizes the importance of cultural issues whenever a firm is evaluating acquisition candidates, as well as having a well-organized transition and ongoing communication to start everything off on the best foot.

SAYS DANIELS:

I think one of the most overlooked aspects in any acquisition is culture. If there isn't a fit at the excitement stage when people want to be a part of something that's bigger, it's not going to come later. The "dating period" is so crucial to getting to know each other from a professional and a personal standpoint. You need to determine if these are people who understand how you think and who can thrive in your environment.

It's also important to recognize that integration can take time. It's worth having a dedicated transition team responsible for the various aspects of introducing new staff members to how you do things at your firm. Of course, you'll want to have associates from the acquired firm involved in the process too. You need to have a pretty detailed script, which should include clearly defined processes, planning worksheets, and so on. Regardless of firm size in an acquisition, you need to go through the same steps—it just might take a bit longer to complete everything with a larger firm.

"There is so much to be concerned about beyond the financials of a deal. Finding a complementary culture, having a successful integration, and creating a better business to serve your clients should be paramount." SHERRI DANIELS

Client and employee communication should be high on the list for the transition team. Open communication is essential for everyone to feel they are in touch with what's happening. Managing expectations is also key, and you need to set realistic time frames for the completion of different tasks, as you'll lose credibility if you keep missing deadlines.

I think we all believe that high performance isn't about the size of a firm in terms of the number of employees or AUM. It's about running a business like a business, providing the services clients expect at a reasonable fee, and making a difference in their lives. Combining resources with other firms, in the right circumstances, can enhance the client experience and create a greater organization.

Key Insight

Growth for growth's sake isn't a viable business practice. Acquisitions should round out your ability to serve clients well and make a true difference in their lives.

[1.2]

CONNECTING THE DOTS

CONSIDER M&A TRANSACTIONS

As these RIA stories show, inorganic growth can bring together like-minded firms and add to your bench strength and geographic coverage. Transactions aren't for the fainthearted, though, and require a lot of time, skill, and money. If this is something you would like to pursue as a buyer, consider some of the following steps to get you started:

Identify Your Ideal Target

Start by clearly outlining the attributes that define an ideal target to keep you focused on the most appropriate candidates. Don't forget about the importance of organic growth at targeted firms, as it can say a lot about a firm's strength and sustainability.

Refine Your Story

To capture the attention of other teams, you'll need to be able to describe your firm's long-term vision, culture, and competitive differentiators, and the reason you think you are an attractive option. Consider capturing your story in a concise pitch book that emphasizes why you are pursuing an expansion strategy, what you hope to achieve, and what the benefits will be for the selling firm. The pitch book should also touch on the financial opportunity, the type of deal structures your firm is open to considering, and your future plans in terms of how you'll help the combined business grow.

You should also be prepared to address a number of related questions. For example:

- Where do you see the points of leverage?
- How would you describe your management style?
- How do you see integration taking place?
- What steps will be taken to align compensation structures and benefit plans?

Assess Scalability

Having the ability to efficiently scale with the addition of new advisors, clients, and assets will be critical. There should be robust, streamlined, and automated capabilities in place—from onboarding procedures to portfolio management, reporting, client service, and more.

Organize Your Support Group

You'll also need to line up people to move efficiently through the different stages of an expansion initiative. On the external side, you might consider hiring an accountant to minimize taxes for both parties, a lawyer to advise on the best corporate structure, and a compliance specialist to ensure that your Form ADV and disclosures are handled properly.

Most importantly, recognize that it's hard to do this on your own. Consider hiring a transaction advisor who understands the complexities of this industry, and can run an end-to-end process with clear steps and milestones. Also speak to peers in the industry, your custodian, and investment bankers to get a sense of the fees involved with hiring external resources, so you can assess these expenditures relative to the benefits you expect to see when a deal closes.

Investigate the Financial Side

Be aware that there are different levers that can be used to structure a deal. These typically include cash paid at the time of closing; seller-financed notes; deferred payments; and/or equity that may take the form of grants, swaps, or employee stock options. You should become familiar with the possible routes, be flexible, and decide in advance what's negotiable and what isn't.

Understand the Valuation

Because the hard assets of an RIA firm are generally minimal, what's really being sold is the cash flow the client base produces. Given this, the business valuation will likely reflect such things as the mix between fees and commissions, the historical organic growth rate of the firm, the age and location of clients, and the staff's experience and tenure. In addition, the valuation and deal value may vary depending on how things are balanced between the buyer and the seller. For example, if risk is shifted to the buyer because it can provide a higher-than-normal percentage of cash up front, this may drive the price down, which would typically be reflected in smaller earnouts on the back end. Alternatively, if the seller takes on more risk in the form of deferred payments, the price may increase accordingly.

 **Go to begreater.com to access additional resources supporting Chapter 1.**

Diversify to Strengthen the Balance Sheet and Reach New Markets

Learn About

- Capitalizing on natural extensions to your business
- Strategies for reaching new investors
- Why digital advice is shaking up the market

As RIAs look to accelerate growth, we are also seeing them add new lines of business that draw on the core competencies of the firm. These include initiatives that expand the service offering for existing clients, as well as initiatives aimed at totally new segments.

In some instances, this diversification is in response to an attractive opportunity. In others, it's a deliberate strategy to create financial strength and resilience to help the firm withstand inevitable ups and downs in the market. The stories that follow show how six RIAs have taken steps to introduce new capabilities.

"Every prudent business needs to diversify. It's what we tell our clients." ADAM BIRENBAUM, CEO
BUCKINGHAM ASSET MANAGEMENT AND BAM ADVISOR SERVICES

PURSUE NATURAL EXTENSIONS

Adam Birenbaum saw opportunities to apply the skills at Buckingham Asset Management to retirement plans, nonprofits, and endowments, creating growth opportunities while helping to balance the business.

SAYS BIRENBAUM:

"We have ventured into new areas that all align with the strengths and expertise of our firm." ADAM BIRENBAUM

Expanding into the retirement space was a natural move for us. Our clients are all connected to a business in some way—whether they are an owner or work for a company—so a lot of wealth is tied to a retirement plan. We were providing counsel to clients on this front as part of the overall relationship, and realized we could also help the retirement providers. We formed Buckingham Retirement Solutions to offer fiduciary services to 401(k), 403(b), and profit-sharing plans, plus professionally managed portfolios and personalized advice for plan participants.

Before we did this, we spent a lot of time and energy looking at what was needed to enter the space. We reviewed the competition, the services they were providing, and where we felt we could differentiate ourselves and make a mark. As we often do, we found a wonderful young person who was passionate about the retirement space and about creating something—and we let him run with it. Today, it's a thriving business. It's also a great aid in discussions with firms looking to join forces with us and wanting to provide additional services to their clients.

The not-for-profit and endowment space was also a natural extension for us. We now have extensive experience serving community foundations, continuing care facilities, private schools, and cultural institutions. We help craft Investment Policy Statements, consult on spending plans, and educate board members on investing and fiduciary responsibilities. It's a good fit for us, and it has also created more business for our traditional wealth management services. People learn more about what we do and become interested in solutions that address their personal needs.

Key Insight

Naturally, you should do what you do best. There may be opportunities to apply your strengths to new areas of the market, however, where you can leverage your core competencies to expand the business.

RESPOND TO CHANGING INVESTOR NEEDS

Peter Raimondi saw a lot of cautious investors after the 2008 downturn. Banyan Partners responded by creating a new line of business that offers investment strategies that move money into cash in a bear situation.

SAYS RAIMONDI:

When we formed our company, our vision was to do something unique and create a place where people could get complete customization of their investment portfolio with in-house resources. Given this, we have high minimums. We were asked if we could also build custom portfolios for clients who were being cautious and wanted to start with smaller investments. The answer, unfortunately, was no.

"Coming out of the financial crisis, people were worried about losing money. We created an attractive alternative for smaller investments." PETER RAIMONDI

I didn't want to confuse the fact that Banyan is for a higher-net-worth client who doesn't want to use model portfolios. So we created an offering that provides a series of tactical ETF-based solutions under a separate brand. It has a different logo and color scheme, and is called Lotus. Since then, we have created a range of strategies, each with its own branding to show they stand apart from one another and address distinct client needs. [You'll hear more about Banyan's product lines in Chapter 4 on client engagement.]

Key Insight

Changing market conditions can impact how people think about investing. Creative responses may open the door to new lines of business that address a different need in the market.

LEVERAGE DIGITAL ADVICE

Steve Lockshin, Founder and Principal of AdvicePeriod and Chairman of Convergent Wealth Advisors, believes that aspects of the investment management process have become commoditized, providing an opportunity for technology to handle these activities more efficiently and at a much lower fee.

SAYS LOCKSHIN:

Investment management is becoming increasingly automated as a growing number of online financial advice providers come to market. Several forces are driving this trend. First of all, technology is at a point where it's very inexpensive to rent computer space and test, test, test. Then you have folks new to the industry who excel at math, understand technology, and recognize the opportunity for digital advice given the degree of commoditization that's taking place in the investment management process, and inevitable fee compression.

> "Looking ten years out, digital advice will be moving at such a pace that by the time it reaches the advisors who aren't tech savvy, it will be too late for them." STEVE LOCKSHIN

Not surprisingly, a number of different firms have taken shape that use technology to handle money management, and more are popping up every day. One is Betterment, which was founded in 2008 and looks to make investing simple. A user's money is placed in a range of goal-based investment portfolios, and additional software helps to harvest tax losses, facilitate transfers, set allocations, and get real-time performance analysis across all goals with one login. The experience is further streamlined with automatic deposits, rebalancing, and reinvestment of dividends.

Will digital advice shake up the market? I don't see it happening in the next few years, but I'm betting it will down the road. I believe digital and traditional advisors will ultimately coexist, and I am working on a new line of business with Betterment to capitalize on the opportunity. It's a platform that will enable advisors to serve their clientele much more efficiently while doing what advisors do best, which is adding the human element to the relationship.

I believe value is created in the advice component where one acts as a true counselor for clients, and that advisors who aren't creating this value will eventually be moved out of the business. My latest venture, AdvicePeriod, is built on this belief. It's a true fiduciary business centered on advice that leverages technology wherever possible to maximize efficiencies, and outsources the more commoditized investment management services.

Key Insight

Technology may be able to handle many parts of the investment management process in an efficient and cost-effective manner. With digital and traditional advice working hand in hand, advisors should have more time for higher-value interactions with clients.

REACH THE UNDERSERVED

Marty Bicknell, CEO of Mariner Holdings, wanted to create a cost-effective way to deliver financial planning to all who come. The firm launched FirstPoint Financial in response, which combines self-service questionnaires, model portfolios, and other techniques.

SAYS BICKNELL:

Our firm has never had account minimums. The number of individuals we were working with who had lower investable assets than our typical high-net-worth client grew to a point where we made a conscious decision to build a dedicated organization that can serve them well. This is FirstPoint Financial, a venture that provides financial planning for clients of all sizes.

"FirstPoint Financial is providing truly personal advice, products, and services previously reserved exclusively for the ultra-high-net-worth investor." MARTY BICKNELL

This isn't a digital-advice concept, but we use technology in a different way. New clients can go to the FirstPoint Web site and complete a questionnaire that provides general information about their financial situation. This is followed up by a phone or in-person discussion with an advisor. The use of technology and model portfolios will help make this a cost-effective venture. In addition, the relationships should be less complicated than with high-net-worth clients, making them easier to handle.

Key Insight

Mass-affluent clients can face different issues from the high-net-worth, and may require an alternative approach to advice as a result. A new delivery model may be a better solution to address their specific needs.

IMPROVE PROFITABILITY

Rick Buoncore, Managing Partner of MAI Wealth Advisors, introduced a money management line of business to complement the firm's wealth management arm.

SAYS BUONCORE:

We have two lines of business: wealth management, where we are independent advisors, and proprietary money management. Our approach to wealth management is very comprehensive, and it takes a lot of work to bring on another multimillion-dollar family. It's much different with the proprietary business, where we can grow more rapidly and with fewer resources.

"We use our proprietary money management service with clients if the offering meets a unique need or provides a cost advantage." RICK BUONCORE

This diversification is helping with the profitability of our firm, and will support continual investment in the overall business. We are in the early stages of looking for external distribution channels for our money management capabilities, and we'll work with consultants to identify attractive opportunities.

Key Insight

It takes a lot of time to bring on a new ultra-high-net-worth client given the usual complexities of these relationships. Additional business lines may introduce a way to expand the client base at a faster pace and with fewer resources.

CAPITALIZE ON OPPORTUNITIES TO ADD TALENT

Richard Burridge, Founding Partner, CEO, and Chief Investment Officer of RMB Capital, highlights the firm's four complementary lines of business: wealth management, asset management, alternative investments, and retirement plan consulting.

SAYS BURRIDGE:

In the beginning, our firm focused on traditional wealth management, while providing in-house investment solutions as well as relevant third-party products. As we grew, our asset management practice established itself as a viable stand-alone business that could serve institutional investors.

In addition, we have an alternative investments platform that we feel enables us to deliver more oversight and transparency of hedge funds. We designed this line of business to attract high-quality hedge fund managers who want to focus on investments only and have us handle other responsibilities — like back-office functions, raising capital, and servicing clients.

"Getting into new lines of business, like hedge funds and retirement plan consulting, was the result of coming across the right people we could add to our team." RICHARD BURRIDGE

Finally, we have a retirement planning business that's relatively new. We came across a retirement plan consulting team that we really admired and felt shared our approach to business. Because we had been collecting a lot of information about our clients' plans in order to advise them on their asset allocation strategies, we thought we could take this further with the right people. We acquired the consulting team, now RMB Retirement Plan Solutions, which works directly with plan providers to help them lower costs and improve services. This also helps us expand the services we are able to offer to our wealth management clients who are business owners with plans or who have company-sponsored plans, and they have really embraced the idea. [You'll hear more about RMB's retirement business in Chapter 3 on technology.]

Key Insight

You may have to find outside talent to expand your business into new areas. Look for people who share your beliefs and operating style and who can bring relevant experience to the table.

[1.3]

CONNECTING THE DOTS

DIVERSIFY THE BUSINESS

This last set of stories points out many different examples of how RIAs are expanding their lines of business. If you are thinking about diversification, consider the following:

- Are you vulnerable today if there is another market downturn? If so, why?
- What would you hope to achieve by adding a new line of business, and how would this support your long-term plan for growth?
- Have you identified potential new business opportunities that are natural extensions of your wealth management practice, or areas where you believe the market is underserved?
- What would it take to be a viable player in these areas? What might competition look like down the road?
- Are you prepared to acquire capabilities, or do you have the expertise internally to support a new line of business?
- How would adding a new line of business affect how your clients view the firm?
- How would this addition affect your current staffing model and how you service existing clients?
- Would there be possible conflicts of interest and, if so, how would you address them?

Go to begreater.com to access additional resources supporting Chapter 1.

As we have seen, RIAs are pursuing many different routes as they look to capitalize on opportunities presented by the changing business environment. Creative partnering, thoughtful mergers and acquisitions, and innovative new ventures are a sign of the times. It will be important to keep a close eye on the evolving competitive landscape and new investor expectations as you assess your options.

In the next chapter, we look at how firms are embracing strategic and succession planning to stay on top of their key priorities.

[2]

Planning Creates Focus to Drive Success

67%

The percentage of advisors without a succession plan ready for implementation*

*The 2013 Fidelity RIA Benchmarking Study was conducted between May 1 and June 28, 2013, in collaboration with an independent third-party research firm unaffiliated with Fidelity Investments. The experiences of the RIAs who responded to the study may not be representative of other RIAs and aren't an indication of future success. A total of 324 firms completed the study.

Planning

"A man who does not plan long ahead will find trouble right at his door." CONFUCIUS

Having plans and committing to them is critical for firms that want to drive change and align their organizations. Among other things, plans can help you focus on achieving long-term goals, acquiring and retaining clients, keeping technology infrastructure up to date, and transitioning the business to new ownership. Surprisingly, many RIAs aren't as committed to planning as we would expect. For an industry that prides itself on helping clients prepare for the future, it seems ironic that advisors aren't heeding their own advice. In this chapter, we discuss two types of plans to help you (1) chart your firm's long-term course, and (2) hand over the reins to a new generation of leaders.

Chart Your Firm's Long-Term Course

Achieving meaningful gains in growth and efficiency requires a vision, organizational alignment, and disciplined execution. Prioritization of initiatives is imperative given the vast spectrum of areas in which you can focus your attention.

Learn About

- Techniques for setting strategic priorities
- Keeping initiatives on track
- Getting staff engaged in the process

It's actually possible to develop a simple, but useful, plan in just a few days that can help you stay on top of what you are trying to achieve, and influence where your business ends up. This roadmap can also facilitate accountability, because many staff members will have responsibility for implementing it, and they'll be evaluated on their success. The four stories that follow show different approaches RIAs are taking as they establish priorities for the firm.

"What you get out of planning can be fantastic—if you are committed to it." GREG ERWIN, CO-FOUNDER AND PARTNER
SAPIENT PRIVATE WEALTH MANAGEMENT

ESTABLISH PRIORITIES

Russ Hill, Chairman and CEO of Halbert Hargrove Global Advisors, conducts strategic planning in a similar way each year, so everyone knows what to expect. A highly disciplined approach to monitoring progress keeps the firm on point to meet its objectives, and active involvement of the entire staff creates a high level of enthusiasm for the process.

SAYS HILL:

I got involved with strategic planning when I was doing volunteer work with a hospital and an aquarium in our area. I saw firsthand how their structured and disciplined approach made a difference, so I brought these ideas to our firm. We now have a formal planning process that involves all our employees. We use a pyramid to outline our major areas of focus, and a tracking spreadsheet to stay on top of everything we have decided to do.

> "Our employees love how we do strategic planning. They know what's going on, what we are trying to do, and what they are supposed to do. They are fully engaged." RUSS HILL

The pyramid contains a series of building blocks:

- The bottom layer is made up of people and culture, investment discipline/wealth advisory services, and financial resilience.
- The middle layer is made up of client experience and leadership/structure.
- The top layer is made up of market differentiation/growth.

With the pyramid, you have to finish the base layer before you can move up. So if you don't have your culture established, investment and wealth advisory services in place, or financial resilience, you aren't ready to think about how to manage the client experience or build leadership. By using the same components in the pyramid year after year, people know how things are going to work together, and how the initiatives we decide on align with the different categories.

We then monitor everything through a color-coded spreadsheet, or scorecard, that shows whether we are on track or not. The spreadsheet itemizes the components of the pyramid and matches the agreed-upon initiatives with each one. Some of the initiatives are evolutionary—you have been doing something and it leads to the next project—and others are based on new ideas. The spreadsheet also captures details about who is responsible for each initiative and the time frame for specific deliverables, and it resides on our intranet, where all the staff can see it.

We never want to get to December and realize we have missed something, so we hold a lot of company meetings throughout the year to discuss our objectives and progress. Our people hold themselves accountable to a high level, and are always looking at the spreadsheet. They point out areas for improvement, where we may need additional resources, or where someone may need to do more. I think if you involve people in important work, then they really like their job and are active contributors. [You'll hear more about how Halbert Hargrove attracts and retains top talent in Chapter 5 on building strong teams.]

Key Insight

To be impactful, a strategic plan needs the support of your staff. Get people involved in helping to shape the initiatives using a process they understand and appreciate. Keep your goals front and center, have your team take ownership for making things happen, and track your progress for all to see.

GATHER INPUT FROM STAFF

Greg Erwin says strategic planning at Sapient Private Wealth Management is a collaborative effort. The executive team gathers input from people at all levels of the organization about what is and isn't working well, and uses this to help establish the firm's priorities.

SAYS ERWIN:

Our five-year objective is to make Sapient the most respected wealth management firm in the Pacific Northwest—not the biggest, but the most respected. We need a roadmap to do that, and that starts with getting input from our staff about how well we are doing and how we can make our firm better.

Every year, I have several review meetings with each person to discuss what we are trying to accomplish, and where there may be obstacles in our way. For example, people may have concerns that we can't meet our goals because we don't have the right technology tools in place, and that's really critical for me to know.

"We took steps to fine-tune our approach to strategic planning. Now there is more clarity and accountability for the entire team, and people are really connected to what we are trying to do." GREG ERWIN

In our annual planning session, we discuss what I have heard and the actions we are going to take as a result. This helps us zero in on our priorities. We may end up with ten things we are going to attack, each with clear descriptions of what we are going to do and who is going to be involved. That dovetails nicely with everyone's individual responsibilities.

In reality, it's easy to lose momentum with your goals—you can hit a bump in the road and get distracted. We are taking steps to make sure that activities are grounded in our overall mission and plan, and that we complete what's critical for our success.

Goals are created for employees in conjunction with senior management and are shared with the entire staff. This way, everyone knows what the operations team has to do, what the research team has to do, and so on, so we can keep each other on point. The goals are also tied to bonuses, so there is a clear financial impact if they are missed. Every other month, each employee has a fifteen-minute check-in with me or his or her manager to review what's been done. It's all about pinpointing obstacles to achieving the objectives, and figuring out how we are going to move ahead.

Key Insight

Good ideas can come from anyone in the organization. Spread your net wide to gather useful input for your strategic plan, show people their views count, and underscore the importance of having the entire team centered on making your goals a reality.

STAY FOCUSED ON WHAT MATTERS

Adam Birenbaum and the senior team at Buckingham Asset Management took time to identify what they saw as opportunities and challenges facing the business in the coming years. This resulted in the creation of four overarching themes that drive the firm's strategic initiatives.

SAYS BIRENBAUM:

I think a firm that performs well is one that's extremely focused, and that's how we measure ourselves. Our leadership team got together and listed all the things we could do to move our business forward—along with all the challenges we could see over the coming years. We had hundreds of bullet points, but started seeing trends.

"When we were formed twenty years ago, the goal was to reach a hundred million dollars in AUM. We'll be close to twenty-five billion in collective assets in 2014. That kind of growth calls for a disciplined way of thinking about the future." ADAM BIRENBAUM

We realized everything fit nicely into four broad categories: (1) attracting and developing top talent, (2) having an unrivaled client experience, (3) developing a robust infrastructure, and (4) having financial strength. We agreed that if we concentrated on these four pillars, we would be one of the recognized leaders in the independent wealth management space.

We define the pillars in the following way:

- **Top talent** is about having a thriving, service-oriented culture. It also includes active and purposeful recruitment to help intelligently plan for growth and succession.
- An **unrivaled client experience** centers on well-defined sets of client interactions that are delivered consistently across all offices and all lines of business.
- A **robust infrastructure** supports integrated systems and processes that make an advisor's life easier so he or she can spend more time on client-facing activities.
- **Financial strength** enables us to capitalize on opportunities to provide resilience and the ability to make ongoing investments in the organization.

Let's look at the client experience as an example. As an RIA gets bigger, it's no longer about interactions with an individual advisor, but interactions with the firm. It's important to take the time to define and articulate the firm-level client experience you want to have. As new offices are opened and new lines of business are introduced, you need to keep this consistent. That's a critical component of being a leader in this space.

Last year we hired a chief marketing officer. One of the first things I tasked him with was learning, defining, and articulating our client experience. While much of what we were doing was consistent across the firm, he found areas where there were variations among our advisors. Through his efforts, we have now laid out a client experience map that our advisors can embrace. Anyone new to the firm can readily see this is the Buckingham way.

A valuable lesson is to create consistency without making the experience too generic. There has to be an element of flexibility and freedom for advisors to customize and personalize things as appropriate. You have to be careful not to over-automate or overengineer this. [You'll hear about other initiatives Buckingham has under way to address the four pillars in later chapters.]

Key Insight

You may have numerous initiatives you are tackling throughout the year. To simplify things, bucket them in three or four main categories to create overarching themes to keep the organization focused on priorities for its success.

SET A NEW DIRECTION

Michael Nathanson brought in a professional facilitator to get the executive team at The Colony Group brainstorming and sharing ideas about the company's future. Together, the executives wrote the firm's strategic plan, and are now actively involved in implementing it to drive change.

SAYS NATHANSON:

After our merger with Mintz Levin Financial Advisors, our executive committee came together to discuss next steps and we brought in a professional facilitator to help us through the process. This person started by interviewing people at all levels within the firm to get a sense of what they thought our value proposition was, and how we were doing overall. When she met with the executive team for a brainstorming session, she had this as background information to make sure we were aligned with our staff.

"After we merged with Mintz Levin Financial Advisors, we knew we needed to revisit our strategic plan." MICHAEL NATHANSON

During the session, we talked about our mission and vision. Then we asked, "Strategically, what do we all think we need to do?" We discussed integrating the newly merged firms, honing our investment process, and improving business development. We had a pretty good idea about all of this, but it was great to get together and express it to each other. This became the basis for our strategic plan.

Our plan is a five-year view, which we'll revisit as circumstances dictate. It's hard to rigorously adhere to it because things change, but once you have gone through the process and have buy-in, you have to follow through as much as possible. I frequently find myself referring to the plan to see if my actions are consistent with the direction we laid out.

Key Insight

The senior team should have a shared view about the company's mission and vision. Bring executives together to discuss and debate your key goals to get everyone on the same page and actively engaged in shaping and implementing your strategic plan.

ASSIGN RESPONSIBILITY FOR CHANGE

Bob Glovsky took responsibility along with another colleague for overseeing the business development elements of The Colony Group's strategic plan.

SAYS GLOVSKY:

When we left the brainstorming session, each of us took ownership of an area and filled out that part of the strategic plan. For example, investment performance was assigned to our chief investment officer, business development was assigned to a colleague and me, and accountability was assigned to Michael. On accountability, each partner has goals related to the plan that get reviewed annually.

"I don't know how an organization can maximize its potential and grow without a strategic plan that sets the direction and assigns responsibility for change." BOB GLOVSKY

One of my initiatives is to help change our culture to one that embraces business development by all—something a lot of people aren't comfortable doing. With our plan in place, employees are now being trained and they are learning how to network and ask for referrals. Our compensation plan will reward them for their successes.

Ongoing communication is obviously essential. Early on in the process, the executive team touched base every two weeks to review the status of various initiatives. Now we do it once a month. Then there are activities with the entire staff, like regular meetings to discuss what people have done to generate business. We are using this in a positive way to look at success stories, wins, and lessons learned.

Key Insight

Every strategic initiative in your plan will need well-defined projects and tactics to help you meet your goals. Assign responsibility for oversight and follow through, and review your progress on a regular basis to assess where tasks stand and any changes you may need to implement to keep things on track.

[2.1]

CONNECTING THE DOTS

CREATE A STRATEGIC PLAN

The RIA stories provide a number of useful takeaways to think about as you look at charting your firm's long-term course. While some advisors feel strategic planning can be a complex and time-consuming process, it doesn't have to be difficult. For example:

1. **Develop or refine your mission, value, and vision statements** to paint a picture of what your firm does and what you aspire to be in the future to serve as a guide for your ongoing decision making.
2. **Understand your current environment** so you know your starting point in terms of the clients you serve today, what the competition looks like, and the products and services you provide.
3. **Evaluate your business** to understand some of the opportunities and challenges you face to help pinpoint priorities for your plan.
4. **Select strategic initiatives and identify projects and tactics** to respond to the opportunities and challenges you have identified, and assign responsibility for carrying out activities.
5. **Establish measurement and tracking parameters** to help monitor the progress that's being made and determine if additional steps need to be taken to move projects and tactics along at a faster pace.
6. **Document your strategic plan** by pulling together the information generated from working through examples 1 through 5 into a concise summary that can be shared with your staff.

As you develop your plan, consider:

- The resources you'll need to execute it, both from an HR and a financial perspective
- Who on your staff has the appropriate skill sets to help move things forward
- How you can combine responsibility with authority to empower people to take action
- How frequently you'll involve staff members to review your long-term goals, progress to date, and potential roadblocks

Be sure to keep things flexible enough to be able to make adjustments along the way as the environment or internal needs change. Also consider revisiting your plan every two years or so to ensure that it continues to adequately capture what you want to achieve.

Go to begreater.com to access additional resources supporting Chapter 2.

Hand Over the Reins to a New Generation of Leaders

Learn About

- Different routes for creating a succession plan
- The traits of leaders
- Bringing in talent from the outside
- Working alongside a successor

You may have spent years building a business, and a well-thought-out plan can help you successfully monetize it when you decide to exit. Of course, it goes without saying that a plan can protect the long-term value of the firm by helping to minimize any disruptions to clients, employees, and the overall operations.

Succession typically involves one of three routes. Business owners can (1) merge or sell the firm to a third party while remaining actively involved, (2) sell to a third party and gracefully exit, or (3) transition it to internal successors. Internal transition was the preferred method identified by more than half (57%) of advisors who participated in the 2013 Fidelity RIA Benchmarking Study. If you are thinking about your next phase of life, see what you can learn from RIAs who chose to sell and stay involved, and from those who chose to transition to an internal successor.

"Forget the turnover of wealth among investors. The turnover of wealth among advisors over the next ten years is going to be industry changing."

ADAM BIRENBAUM, CEO
BUCKINGHAM ASSET MANAGEMENT
AND BAM ADVISOR SERVICES

SELL AND STAY INVOLVED

SEEK GROWTH

Bob Glovsky says his previous firm, Mintz Levin Financial Advisors, found a strong partner with a common culture in The Colony Group, providing a succession plan for the firm and good long-term career opportunities for the staff.

SAYS GLOVSKY:

Succession had been on our minds for a while. We told our people we were cognizant of the issue and were coming up with a solution that we fundamentally believed was in their best interests, and in the best interests of our clients. Of course, that was the merger with The Colony Group.

We knew we needed to find a firm that understood the RIA space, had a fiduciary model, was committed to wealth management, and meshed with our culture. This was a perfect match, and the willingness of people to work together since the merger has been great. The old Mintz Levin team has tremendous respect for the management at Colony, and appreciates what this change can offer career-wise. In fact, five of them have been named partners of the firm.

Key Insight

A merger can serve as an efficient succession plan by aligning your firm with a younger team that will be with the business for a long period of time. If you are considering this route, get your staff involved early on and excited about the new possibilities this can present in terms of expanded capabilities for the firm and additional career opportunities.

TRANSITION TO AN INTERNAL SUCCESSOR

ACCESS FINANCING

Bob DiQuollo chose to have Brinton Eaton Wealth Advisors join Mariner Wealth Advisors to hand off time-consuming back-office functions to an array of specialists and to obtain access to financing the next generation of management needed to execute a succession plan.

SAYS DIQUOLLO:

We had a succession plan in place, but after the financial crisis of 2008 our growth had slowed. This had implications for the finances the younger members of our team had available to buy out the older advisors who would be leaving the firm at some point. Doing a deal with Mariner Wealth Advisors provided, and will provide, the necessary funds to help facilitate this transfer of ownership and any future transfers. Naturally, our staff was very pleased that current owners would still be partial owners and that there could be opportunities to be a replacement for people as they retired. When we told our clients what we were doing, they were also pleased to hear we were planning for the future.

"We had the right people on board who could take over management of the firm at some point—but they didn't have the buying power." BOB DIQUOLLO

I think joining Mariner will also help us attract new people as we look to grow. Recruits will be able to see a very stable firm with a strong investor backing us, and a broader set of opportunities now that we are part of a larger network.

Key Insight

Advisors who have built a strong business will be looking to monetize it when they are ready to retire. Strategic partners can help support this by providing financing options for successors to help them with their buyout strategies.

GROOM FUTURE LEADERS

Adam Birenbaum and his team at Buckingham Asset Management have clearly articulated the attributes of a leader at the firm, and they take well-defined steps to develop the skills necessary to have an effective next generation of management.

SAYS BIRENBAUM:

In order to set up our clients for long-lasting success, we knew we needed a well-defined succession plan. The senior men and women in our firm met to discuss what constitutes a leader at Buckingham, and we identified six success criteria: (1) high personal standards, (2) embraces the culture, (3) entrepreneurial, (4) good thinker, (5) wants to learn, and (6) people oriented.

> "It seemed like we had grown up in the blink of an eye and had to plot the next chapter in our history." ADAM BIRENBAUM

Each of these criteria encompasses a number of additional attributes. For example, we think personal standards include operating at the highest level of integrity and trust, and not accepting mediocrity. We think entrepreneurial includes taking initiative to make things happen, and constantly looking for the next good idea. All this gives our people guidance on the types of behaviors—not skills, but behaviors—that make someone a great leader.

Leadership takes many forms and we believe that anyone, from our newest to most seasoned folks, can provide leadership. I experienced this firsthand, becoming CEO of the firm when I was just 32 years old. What a testament to an organization that would be willing to put such a young person in charge, while at the same time providing the support, structure, development, and mentoring to make sure things worked out.

We spend a great deal of time on associate development. Each person is reviewed annually and receives feedback on how he or she is doing relative to the defined leadership attributes. There is also an advanced program that takes high-potential management candidates through all the key elements of the company, including governance, finance, and decision making. These people are invited to join meetings with the operating committee, board of managers, and other groups to get a closer view of the workings of the firm.

Key Insight

Articulating the traits of leaders can help staff members understand what's required to make the grade, and give them something to aspire to. Use these traits to guide your selection of promising management talent, and develop programs that can expose them to different aspects of the business to build their knowledge and skills.

BRING IN AN EXTERNAL SUCCESSOR

Jane Williams, Chair and Co-Founder of Sand Hill Global Advisors, took steps to put ownership into the hands of the firm's employees, and then looked externally to complement the team with additional management talent.

SAYS WILLIAMS:

When my partner and one other senior person started discussing retirement, I knew it would be difficult to transfer ownership internally given the lack of available liquidity. The younger professionals in the firm were just starting to raise families and buy their first homes, and there was no real financing in the marketplace at the time. I faced a dilemma: While I needed to pay my retiring colleagues, I also needed to replace the knowledge that would be leaving the firm with their departure. If I used my own finances to buy them out, I would have less on hand to rebuild the professional staff. I decided we needed to find a buyer.

"In the late 1990s, two senior people at our firm began speaking about retiring. This put the sustainability challenge front and center for me." JANE WILLIAMS

We put out a few feelers about selling, and received several bids, but ended up withdrawing ourselves from the market. Then we were approached by a bank that spoke our language, so we sold to them in 2000 and became an autonomous, wholly owned unit of the company.

We had a good relationship with our acquirer, but felt we couldn't make a major impact on their business. We also wanted control over what was going to happen next. We discussed our situation with the CEO of the bank, who was very supportive of our desire for change. Then we explored financing arrangements that would let us buy Sand Hill back.

In the end, we decided to work with Fiduciary Network, a company interested in long-term, income-generating investments. This appealed to me because it's a passive arrangement without any day-to-day involvement in our operations. The financing is permanent, consisting of a note convertible into nonvoting equity. For RIAs of our size with a long history, there will likely be a partner who needs to step aside at some point. If a founder lends money to successors, I feel it doesn't shift the responsibility or risk.

With the help of Fiduciary Network, we initially bought back twenty-five percent of our firm, and then the remainder over time. I was able to get four of my colleagues into the first buying group, and then another four into the second. This ownership structure has created a real entrepreneurial spirit at Sand Hill.

I then began a search for external talent. It's very difficult to hire senior-level leaders. It takes a lot of time to identify the right candidate, and then a lot of time getting to know them before they come on board. I did an extensive search for a new chief investment officer: We started with a recruiter who presented us with five or six candidates, but they weren't right for our business. After two years, we were introduced to Brian Dombkowski through someone we knew, and we realized we had a great person in front of us. He quickly became an integral part of our firm.

Over time, it became clear that Brian would become my successor. We have an incredibly collaborative relationship and know how to mine each other's talents for the overall good of the company. I feel we now have the people in place for the firm's long-term sustainability.

Key Insight

You may need to bring an external person into the fold to ultimately be your successor, and it can take time to find the right person and to groom him or her. Having a stake in the business can boost the entrepreneurial spirit, so consider offering equity to your high-potential employees as well as senior executives.

WORK ALONGSIDE A FOUNDER

Brian Dombkowski, CEO and Chief Investment Officer of Sand Hill Global Advisors, became president of the firm and then moved into his current leadership position, taking control of the operational aspects of the business.

SAYS DOMBKOWSKI:

When I joined Sand Hill, the firm was just emerging from its relationship with a bank. It had a great brand, long history, critical mass, and was about to put ownership into the hands of its employees. There is a saying, "No one ever washes a rental car." It's true—ownership matters and creates a wonderful economic incentive for everyone involved. It was a very attractive situation, and I joined as chief investment officer.

> "A successful transition requires a founder ready to hand over responsibility, and a new leader who appreciates the opportunity in front of them." BRIAN DOMBKOWSKI

At the time, I didn't think I was coming in as Jane's successor; rather, my mission was to be as proactive and expansionary as I could be with the investment offering. I tried to lead in a collaborative manner, and I focused on the acquisition and development of talent. Over time, more authority was given to me—finance, client relations, and client service. Somewhere in that evolution, it became evident to Jane and the shareholder group that I was the succession choice. I became president about eighteen months later, and the transition to CEO followed.

Jane and I are partners in every sense of the word. She has exceptional institutional knowledge and a significant reach in our industry, which I find invaluable as we consider any number of business development and strategic matters.

There are a number of things you need to have in place to make working alongside a founder a success. First of all, you need a very thoughtful, well-articulated succession plan. We spent a year developing ours, and it's been an incredible guide. It looked out five years and clearly outlined what needed to happen to get to our end goal. It was very specific about transitioning roles and responsibilities, ownership, and relationships, and how we were going to do it.

You also need at least five years to execute the plan, a strong financing structure to transfer ownership internally, and willing participants—including a founder who is ready to relinquish control and a highly capable next-generation person to take charge. When we speak with other firms, we often see a lack of alignment. The successor may fail to appreciate the opportunity he or she has been given, and the founder may be having difficulty transitioning into this next phase. That's a recipe for disaster. Both sides need to be open, positive, and willing to embrace change.

Fortunately, all this has come together for us. Jane continues to be an extremely valuable resource for the firm. She may choose to stay for a long time, but the infrastructure and training is in place to keep things running smoothly should she decide to wind down at some point.

Key Insight

Executing an internal succession strategy can be a complex and lengthy process, even if you have identified the right individual to take over the firm. A detailed plan that outlines all the changes that will take place at different points in time—including changes to responsibilities, ownership, and compensation—can help make the transition a success.

[2.2]

CONNECTING THE DOTS

CREATE A SUCCESSION PLAN

Different Approaches

As we have seen from these stories, transitioning a business you have spent years building is likely going to take time. Because there are several routes you can take to hand over ownership, it's worth stepping back and determining what you want the next phase of your life to look like to help pinpoint which one suits you best. Ask questions to see which of the following three options you should choose.

1. **Merge or Sell and Stay Involved**
   - I am interested in continuing to work for the foreseeable future.
   - I want to join forces with like-minded advisors.
   - I am interested in realizing a portion of my firm's equity now.
   - I am fully willing to work on merging cultures, staff, marketing, etc.

2. **Transition to an Internal Successor**
   - I have internal staff members with the talent and access to capital to be successors.
   - I am willing to invest several years preparing for the hand-off.
   - I am comfortable handing over the reins to another.
   - I realize that monetizing the business may take longer if I gradually transition ownership.

3. **Sell and Move On**
   - I would like to exit the firm entirely following the earnout period.
   - I am willing to give up my company name and brand.
   - I have prepared my clients and employees for the possibility of new ownership.
   - I realize that some staff members may lose their jobs.

Internal Successors

As we indicated previously, internal transition was the preferred method identified by more than half (57%) of advisors who participated in the 2013 Fidelity RIA Benchmarking Study. If this is the route for you as well, take the time to evaluate your staff to see if you have a potential successor on board today.

Think about your firm's most critical business needs for long-term success and the skills and experience that will be required to effectively address these needs. You might consider some of the following traits in a candidate:

> **Ability to grow the business:** Does this individual know how to generate referrals from existing relationships and have ideas for finding new prospects?
>
> **Management acumen:** How able is he or she to run a business, prioritize issues, and manage day-to-day responsibilities?
>
> **Leadership and people skills:** Can he or she work well with people, generate enthusiasm, and create the balance of accountability and reward?
>
> **Self-knowledge:** Does this individual know what he or she doesn't know, and can turn to others who can fill gaps where necessary?
>
> **Trust:** Do you fully and deeply trust this individual enough to share business issues and personal concerns? (This is, perhaps, the most important factor when considering internal talent.)
>
> **Willingness to take responsibility:** Is he or she willing to take over, step into your shoes, and be fully accountable for the success or failure of the business?

As you consider a potential internal successor, realize that it can take years of grooming for the next generation to be ready to accept the level of responsibility necessary to run a wealth advisory business.

A Transition Plan

If you'll be handing over the business to an internal successor, consider working with them on the details of a transition plan. The plan should look at changes that will take place in three main areas: (1) responsibilities, (2) control/ownership, and (3) compensation.

1. **Responsibilities:** As you begin to wind down, you'll be shedding different responsibilities, and your successor will likely be taking them on. You'll need to consider the speed at which you want this to take place.
2. **Control/ownership:** While giving up control and ownership can be emotionally difficult, you'll need to have a clear picture of how this will happen over time, and the financial structures that will support it.
3. **Compensation:** Your compensation will be affected by the pace at which you transfer responsibilities and control/ownership. You'll need to map this out and assess the financial consequences to fully understand the implications for your cash flow.

Dealing with these issues up front can help eliminate any ambiguity that may exist, and reduce stress levels for you and your successor.

Go to begreater.com to access additional resources supporting Chapter 2.

Charting the course for your firm and developing a succession plan naturally go hand in hand. If someone is in a position to take over the business—whether as an outside acquirer or an internal candidate—he or she will want to know what your long-term vision is and how you expect to put it into practice. A powerful strategy can help motivate people about future prospects, and increase interest in being part of an attractive business.

In the next chapter, we look at how firms are harnessing technology to improve efficiencies, enhance the level of engagement with clients, and drive revenue growth.

[3]

Harnessing Technology Enhances the Client Experience

66%

The percentage of advisors who believe that technology is becoming a key part of their strategy for success*

*The 2013 Fidelity® Advisor Insights study was conducted in collaboration with Bellomy Research, an independent third-party research firm not affiliated with Fidelity Investments. Participants included advisors from across multiple firm types who work primarily with individual investors and manage a minimum of $10 million in individual or household investable assets. Firm types included a mix of banks, broker-dealers, independent broker-dealers, insurance companies, regional broker-dealers, RIAs, and wirehouses, with findings weighted to reflect industry composition. The study was conducted online from August 8, 2013, through August 21, 2013, and included responses from 813 advisors. Fidelity wasn't identified as the sponsor.

Technology

> "There's a way to do it better—find it." THOMAS EDISON

According to the 2013 Fidelity RIA Benchmarking Study, firms recognize the strategic importance of technology, using it to improve efficiency and profitability, enhance their clients' experiences, and support scalable organic growth. Participants in the study were focused primarily on optimizing their current systems—versus investing in new capabilities—by driving initiatives related to integration, workflows, and training. The firms we spoke with have also taken steps to get the most from their existing technology, and are leveraging new solutions as well. As technology continues to quickly evolve and tech-savvy competitors emerge, RIAs realize they need to stay on top of—and embrace—recent developments. In this chapter, we look at how you can effectively harness technology to (1) get your infrastructure right and enhance the client experience, and (2) capitalize on new devices and applications to further support advisor productivity, client satisfaction, and operational effectiveness.

Get Your Infrastructure Right and Enhance the Client Experience

Learn About

- Integration
- Creating a centralized hub
- Workflows
- Features of the cloud
- Different solutions for different lines of business

When RIAs describe their technology platform, they typically discuss systems for financial planning, portfolio management, rebalancing, customer relationship management (CRM), and document storage. The conversation then invariably moves to integration—how each of these systems speaks to one another and enables data to be shared and workflows to be streamlined. After all, by bringing different systems together, integration enhances efficiencies, reduces operational risk, and helps firms be more responsive to their clients. In the 2013 Fidelity RIA Benchmarking Study, 67% of high-performing firms* ranked integrating existing systems as one of their top three opportunities.

> "Technology lets us work more efficiently, and monitor and evaluate how we interact with clients."
>
> JERRY LUFF, CHIEF OPERATING OFFICER BAKERAVENUE

*The term "high-performing firms" refers to the subset of participating firms in the 2013 Fidelity RIA Benchmarking Study with business results that meet the following two sets of criteria. The first is eligibility criteria based on time in the business, AUM, number of employees, and organic growth. The second is performance criteria based on three-year AUM compound annual growth rate, earnings before owner's compensation, and revenue per full-time equivalent—all based on December 31, 2012, numbers. Reference to the concept of "performance" or "performing" isn't intended to connote investment returns.

Beyond integration, RIAs are looking for other ways to leverage technology to streamline business processes and deepen client relationships. These include creating centralized hubs, automating workflows, and adopting hosted applications that sit in the cloud.* The six stories that follow provide insights into some of these activities.

INTEGRATE SYSTEMS TO CREATE A CENTRALIZED HUB

Russ Hill saw the benefits of integration years ago, and Halbert Hargrove Global Advisors took steps to put its own set of linked components in place. Given the money and effort required to keep things going, buying and customizing is the firm's preferred route today.

SAYS HILL:

Integration has always been a priority for us, and in early 2000 we built our own integrated CRM, document management, and publishing system because no one else provided one at the time. In the end, it didn't make economic sense to keep it going, plus it's hard to link this kind of capability with new technologies that come on the market. We now prefer to buy and find a provider that can do the customization for us.

> "The purpose of technology is to enhance productivity and improve interactions for employees and clients alike." RUSS HILL

Our technology team has spent a lot of time reviewing our business processes to determine how best to systematize everything to improve how we operate and interact with clients. Our goal has always been to run as many processes through one application as possible, including client onboarding, client service, reporting, and administration.

*Each client needs to conduct his or her own due diligence, consider the advantages and disadvantages of using cloud-based technology, and determine whether cloud-based technology is the appropriate solution for the firm.

To support this, we have modified an off-the-shelf CRM system that serves as a centralized hub. A great deal of information is automatically driven into the CRM client folders, so everything an externally facing person needs to know is readily available. For example, our trading system integrates with our portfolio management system, which integrates with our CRM, so we can import account information every day. We also use a third-party aggregation service to capture information on held-away assets that may be in an IRA or a 401(k) account.

This centralized approach is helping us analyze our client base more thoroughly. We can look at the ages of all our clients, the key services they use, how many are engaged with us, and what we should do to follow up. This will help us provide a better, more customized experience.

Key Insight

You can build or buy technology, but keep in mind that you'll be responsible for ongoing maintenance if you choose the first route. A centralized hub may take a lot of effort to develop, but it can be well worth it in the end given its positive impact on advisor efficiency and the client experience. Evaluate what's required to support client-facing activities.

INTEGRATE SYSTEMS TO MINIMIZE DATA ENTRY

John Augenblick, President of Rockwood Wealth Management, follows a number of strict rules when it comes to the type of technology the firm uses. Integrated, best-of-breed capabilities are high on the list.

SAYS AUGENBLICK:

We have two overarching rules when it comes to technology. First, all our applications need to talk to one another. I don't want my staff doing data entry in multiple systems, as that opens up opportunities for errors. Second, everything has to be Web based.

> "We don't want our staff involved in any time-consuming activities that don't add a lot of value to client relationships." JOHN AUGENBLICK

There is always the temptation to go with one of the "silver bullet" solutions that are on the market today that purports to do everything—from portfolio rebalancing to trading to CRM and more. Alternatively, you can bring together best-of-breed applications that fit how you do business. I like to be able to choose the best systems for our firm and then link to other providers.

We have a direct download of data from our custodian to our portfolio accounting system, which speaks to our CRM system. Our CRM system is then hooked up to our financial planning software, so no manual data entry is taking place to migrate information from one database to another. We also use a hosted exchange server that archives emails in our CRM, even though we use Microsoft® Outlook® on our desktops. This lets us efficiently retain and retrieve emails as needed for compliance purposes.

I feel that ninety-five percent of the gain that comes from technology is just having the different components in place. All the tinkering you can do might get you another five percent of efficiency when you account for the learning curve and the training that will be needed. It's much better to master what you have than to always be adjusting and changing to the next greatest thing.

Key Insight

Some providers combine multiple applications in one offering. Evaluate the trade-offs of all-inclusive capabilities compared with buying best of breed for each application. If you decide to go with best of breed, determine which providers have standard integration among the components you select. For those providers that don't have standard integration, discuss custom options with them and, if necessary, with outside development consultants as well.

AUTOMATE TOUCH POINTS

Jerry Luff, Chief Operating Officer of BakerAvenue, says one of the ways their team differentiates itself is by the level of service provided to both prospects and clients. The firm has built numerous workflows into its CRM system to ensure that all interactions are top-notch.

SAYS LUFF:

It took us a while to get our technology infrastructure right, and we had several fits and starts before it all came together. Our first attempts were Excel® based, then we moved to an enhanced spreadsheet option, and then to a CRM system that we never had any traction with. We got a little bit better each time, but it wasn't until a new CRM solution came to market in 2009 that we had what we needed. It provided a launching point for our technology backbone.

"We utilize technology to make sure we can deliver what we promise in terms of the prospect and client experience." JERRY LUFF

CRM became the core of our platform. We were small enough at the time that adoption wasn't a problem, and people's commitment grew as they saw how the system could help them do their job better. At the same time, I moved out of my role as an advisor and took over operational responsibilities for the firm. I think having a full-time person dedicated to technology is essential if you are to have the philosophy and systems you need to help create a competitive advantage.

Technology is key to delivering on our firm's promise to prospects and clients. On the sales side, we probably have one hundred and fifty different workflows built into our CRM system to track activity—from when we get a referral to the multiple communications that occur before we turn that lead into a client relationship. With automated prompts for phone calls and emails, we can be confident that the prospect is well taken care of.

The same is done for client service. Thirty days after onboarding, there is a mandatory phone call to see if the client was able to easily access our vault where we keep statements and communications, and if all the information was correct. From there, we discuss how and when the client would like to receive future communications, and the system provides ongoing tracking so we know if staff members are ahead or behind on required tasks.

Workflows are continually being added or removed based on new or changing needs. For example, we introduced a workflow that utilizes a survey app to provide new clients with a brief email that asks how they would rate the interaction with their advisor and the service team, and whether they thought the paperwork and marketing material was effective. It's a great feedback tool, and the information is easy to collect when technology is introduced.

Today, there are a lot of new applications being built for CRM. One automatically brings our email into the system, and continued innovations are linking reporting tools with CRM and providing more updated information on account balances and the like. Soon we'll be linking our CRM and telecommunications system for auto-dial, where a person's information will automatically pop up based on his or her phone number.

The cloud is also a big part of what we do, because it lowers the cost of administration and the need to have expensive technology professionals on staff. It's also good not to have all your eggs in one basket from a disaster-recovery perspective—especially since we are located in San Francisco. Our performance reporting software, email, highly encrypted client vault, and phone system are all cloud based.

Key Insight

Technology is so critical for the success of an RIA that it's worth having a full-time person dedicated to this area. Broad adoption of systems across the firm is also important, especially for CRM, which is only as good as the information that's entered. Automating workflows can have a significant impact on the experience of both prospects and clients, helping to close and retain business.

DO MORE WITH LESS

Doug Couden, Chief Investment Officer of BakerAvenue, believes that the financial services industry has leveraged technology more than many other industries have, making it possible for his team to do numerous tasks with fewer people.

SAYS COUDEN:

I'm in charge of directing the investment process at BakerAvenue, and I manage a group of analysts, traders, and others who work hand in hand with the client service team. I think financial services—in particular asset management and wealth management—has leveraged technology more than many other industries have. From screening to portfolio management to trade reconciliation tools, we have pretty much everything we need on our desktops. This has made the application of our investment approach much more efficient. Where you needed two or three people to provide analytics before, you can now do it with two or three clicks with the right applications.

"Given today's technology, a small trading floor can do pretty much everything a large trading floor could have done ten years ago." DOUG COUDEN

There are many technology providers in the market, so we did a lot of beta testing to identify solutions that met our specific requirements. You need to find capabilities that match what you are trying to accomplish, and some firms and applications were just more in tune with what we wanted to do.

Our central hub of investment activity is our trading floor, where four or five of us sit surrounded by TVs to share ideas and talk about the market. We have another office as well that we hook in via webcasts for different presentations and discussions.

Key Insight

There are many applications available today that can assist with the asset management side of the business, supporting analytics to trading to reporting. Take the time to test different solutions to find the combination that works best for how you handle your investment process.

MAKE A BIG IMPACT WITH SMALL STEPS

Karen Keatley, President and Chief Investment Officer of Keatley Wealth Management, wants her team to work on what matters most for clients, and technology helps eliminate time-consuming tasks from their workday.

SAYS KEATLEY:

We are a small firm and my preference is to keep staffing to a minimum, using our people to their highest ability. As a result, technology plays an important role for us.

> "I want to make sure we are all doing what we do best, and implement technology solutions wherever possible to free up staff time." KAREN KEATLEY

We have implemented a few things that seem small, but are actually large in terms of their impact on our productivity. For example, we have a customized online questionnaire that we use to collect information on a new client, which automatically populates our financial planning software. It's an enormous time saver in terms of data input and accuracy—helping us as well as our clients. We have also implemented a capability that takes data from our CRM system and automatically populates custodial forms. We are always looking for similar ways to improve our processes.

We also outsource some of our technology applications, including the use of our portfolio management and reporting solution that has accounting, reporting, and billing functions all in one. A third-party firm handles the daily downloads of our custodial data into the system, and compiles and maintains the information. They create customized client reports, calculate my fees based on a formula I provide, and generate all my client invoices. I think it's the perfect solution for what we need.

Key Insight

Even small changes can help firms streamline their processes and interactions with clients. Investor-oriented tools, like questionnaires that gather information to populate applications, can help advisory firms connect with clients while also adding efficiencies. Look at time-consuming activities that you may be able to automate and/or outsource to third-party specialists to reduce the workload on your staff.

USE DIFFERENT TECHNOLOGIES FOR DIFFERENT LINES OF BUSINESS

In Chapter 1, we looked at RIAs who are diversifying their business. One such firm is RMB Capital. In 2012, RMB launched its retirement plan consulting business with the help of Walt Melcher, V.P. and Director of RMB Retirement Plan Solutions, which requires a different set of technologies from the firm's wealth management practice area.

SAYS MELCHER:

I have been in the retirement plan business for many years and had launched my own plan advisory firm called ClearPath Retirement Partners. I decided that if I was going to really grow the business, I needed to find a strong partner, so I joined RMB Capital in 2012—and ClearPath became RMB Retirement Plan Solutions.

We leverage some of the same technology applications that are used more widely throughout the firm, like the CRM system, but Retirement Plan Solutions also has unique needs that RMB accommodates by providing us access to two specialized technology resources. One is a third-party application with modules that can be customized to manage our unique data and reporting needs. It helps us with three areas: monitoring fiduciary activities, providing investment due diligence, and benchmarking recordkeeper services and fees. The other is also a third-party application that helps us evaluate how prepared plan participants are for retirement.

"We leverage technology to help our clients drive measurable improvements across all aspects of their retirement plans." WALT MELCHER

With the first application, the module for fiduciary activities lets us conduct a series of compliance checks and track actions on an ongoing basis. There is also a secure, online portal for all the performance reports, checklists, and plan documents, so plan committee members can easily access any information they want related to their responsibilities. The module for investment due diligence lets us provide clients with an assessment of performance against our benchmarks. Finally, the module for benchmarking provides robust recordkeeper analysis and reporting capabilities to collect, evaluate, and compare a wide range of data from many different vendors. This supports a client's need to monitor and benchmark his or her providers to ensure that services and fees are competitive, plus it helps us readily respond to any proposal request that comes up.

By using this third-party application, versus building a capability in house, we save a lot of time and money. In addition, the provider has created data links with some of the major recordkeepers. With this integration, we can view a recordkeeper's data on our clients' plans right from our application, including quarter-end information on investment options and the distribution of assets by each option. We don't have to do manual data entry or file updates, which saves time, reduces errors, and enhances our reporting capabilities.

The application is also cloud based, which is very helpful because I travel a lot. It enables me to show clients reports on a tablet rather than printing them out, which also saves time and money and helps us work toward being a paperless office.

On the participant side, the second application enables us to evaluate employee utilization of a plan by different segments of a client's demographic. For example, how are the employees in the twenty- to thirty-year-old segment saving? How are they investing? Are they on track to achieve their retirement savings goals? These findings help us advise clients on the best strategies to improve areas of deficiency in different parts of the population. We are always on the lookout for new technology like this that can help us bring more value to the table and deepen the way we consult with clients.

Key Insight

If you are thinking about diversifying your business, you'll also need to consider what type of technology systems may be required to operate any new activities efficiently and to meet the specific needs of different types of clients. The retirement plan advisory area calls for capabilities tailored to plan sponsors as well as plan participants.

[3.1]

CONNECTING THE DOTS

LEVERAGE TECHNOLOGY

The RIA stories show that technology can help you transform your business by enabling you to work more efficiently and deepen client engagement. To see where you may be able to gain the greatest benefit from new or upgraded capabilities, take a step back and look at where things aren't running as smoothly as they could be—then ask how technology might help. Before moving ahead with anything new, however, check your readiness for change: Any adjustment can be disruptive if you aren't well prepared.

Check Your Readiness

To help guide your thinking, look at the following four areas:

- **Your business strategy.** Do you have a clear vision of where your firm is headed longer term and why implementing a new system is necessary to meet your overall objectives?
- **Your people.** Is your team ready to embrace a new system, and do they have the time and background to help make it a success?
- **Your processes.** Are your business processes working well today and can they be further automated with a new system?
- **Your existing technology.** Do you see opportunities to reduce redundancies, increase functionality, and enhance integration, which may help you narrow your choices as you review different options?

If the answer is "yes" in each area, you are likely ready for change and should take a close look at what you hope to achieve with new technology. Will integrating different systems, automating business processes, or moving to the cloud help you get where you want to be? The following sections provide detailed information about these three areas, along with things to consider.

Integration

Integration means different things to different providers, so make sure you are on the same page as others when discussing this topic. There are two types of integration: data integration and workflow integration.

Data integration makes it possible for different systems to easily pass information to each other, and includes:

1. **Exports and imports** to download data from a source system into an intermediary format and then upload the data into a destination system
2. **Automated data feeds** that offer a routine way for one system to automatically provide data to another system on a periodic basis, or for bidirectional data flows to take place
3. **Application programming interfaces (APIs) and Web services** that provide a blueprint for programmers to build a bridge between systems to move data back and forth in a secure and automated fashion

Workflow integration lets a user access multiple systems in a highly efficient and user-friendly manner, and includes:

1. **Single sign-on (SSO),** whereby a user logs on to one system and gains secure access to all systems that are part of the integrated platform without being prompted to log on to each of them again
2. **Contextual linking,** where the data you are looking at is directly linked and contextually appropriate in different components of the integrated system; for example, if you are looking at an account in a CRM system and want to see specific information in a custodial platform, you simply click a link that launches that platform via an SSO, taking you directly to the account of interest

As you review integration options, consider the differences between single-vendor and best-of-breed solutions. With single-vendor, one provider has typically built all the core components of a platform and is responsible for ongoing maintenance, management, and client service. By contrast, best-of-breed is an open platform where the provider has integrated with a number of third-party applications in each core technology category, typically enabling you to choose the CRM, financial planning, or other applications that meet your specific needs. This lets each third-party firm focus on its core competencies and integrate with other providers that complement its solution.

Business Process Workflows

Are your business processes loosely documented, leaving staff members to do things instinctively or through course of habit? Taking steps to standardize common tasks using workflows that outline how they should be handled each and every time they are performed can enhance client service, improve efficiency, reduce errors, and help with training new employees.

Workflows can be applicable to many parts of an advisory business, including sales, portfolio management, and operations. If you are beginning to use them, consider taking four steps:

1. **Pick a client-facing set of activities to build out a workflow.** This may be onboarding or some other early-stage interaction that can help set the tone for the entire relationship.
2. **Determine the type of workflow you'll develop.** Ask yourself whether the order is relevant, whether activities will move between different people, and whether the workflow will depend on things happening within a certain time period, as these will dictate the type of workflow you should develop.
3. **Choose the best method to create the workflow.** Get all the stakeholders in a room and use a whiteboard to gather information on steps, resources, time frames, and dependencies. Be sure to review the workflow several times and refine it before it's launched.
4. **Get ready to measure the impact.** Determine how you'll measure the impact of the workflow at the start of the initiative to help underscore the fact that you are expecting to see positive results based on its use by everyone.

Also consider whether you can automate these tasks and their interdependencies in a system to streamline them even further. As you review your business processes, think about your firm's situation related to operational complexity, compliant storage needs, and connectivity to systems of record in order to identify the most appropriate solution. Managing your workflows within a CRM system may or may not be the best answer. A business process management system specifically designed to manage and control workflows may be a better option. There are offerings that combine workflow and document management and that automate, track, and control the way complex work gets done. These sophisticated capabilities may help you be more efficient, reduce costs, better comply with regulations, and improve client service.

Cloud Computing*

In the broadest sense, cloud computing can be described as making use of technology resources that exist beyond the walls of your office environment. So, if your Web server, email server, or any of your software applications are located and managed off site, you are, in a sense, practicing a form of cloud computing.

As we saw in some of the earlier stories, there are many applications that are offered in the cloud today that can increase mobility, lower up-front infrastructure costs, and enable you to outsource technology administration and maintenance. There are even cloud-based virtual offices that integrate all your data and applications for access from one central place. This includes Web apps and hosted Windows®, legacy, and custom software. Imagine being at a conference in another city and needing to deal with a time-sensitive issue that requires accessing files on your desktop. Simply use your tablet to tap into your cloud-based system and get everything you need.

While there can be many benefits to cloud-based applications, the security of cloud providers should be part of a rigorous evaluation process. After all, RIAs operate in a regulatory environment that requires you to safeguard client information, while many cloud-based solution providers may not share those same industry-specific concerns or follow the internal standards articulated by a firm's compliance policies. If you are interested in applications offered in the cloud, you should also review a provider's:

- Redundancy and backup capabilities
- Disaster recovery plan
- Policies regarding confidentiality
- Storage capacity
- Accessibility via mobile applications
- Client support model

Go to begreater.com to access additional resources supporting Chapter 3.

*Each client needs to conduct his or her own due diligence, consider the advantages and disadvantages of using cloud-based technology, and determine whether cloud-based technology is the appropriate solution for the firm.

We also leverage technology to help take our communications strategy to a new level. This requires using a range of media that complement one another. For example, every week we send out an email about what we have seen taking place in the markets, and we use this as an opportunity to tweet about our sentiment.* The tweet may contain a link to our CEO's most recent video on a financial news network, and a link to view archives of his interviews on our Web site. A portfolio manager may then draw on the email, tweet, and video to add content to his or her blog, giving us a lot of mileage for all the content we create.

We have also been combining social media with a more traditional approach for outreach to engage our clients in a fun "give-back" initiative. Last holiday season, we randomly selected a group of clients who each received a ten-dollar gift card† with a note that thanked them for working with our firm. The note said we would like them to give the gift card to someone in need and tell us about the experience on our company blog. The blog let us capture a tremendous outpouring of stories and share them with all our stakeholders. We'll definitely do something like this again.

Our technology team is highly focused on innovation and process improvement. Each person has quarterly goals for qualified enhancements, and there is a process in place for collectively reviewing these and deciding which ones we want to pursue. Choices have to be significant, implementable, and aligned with our firm's ongoing initiatives. Once they are agreed upon, someone owns them and makes sure they work properly.

*Be knowledgeable about regulations regarding social media and your firm's specific policies.

†Know and adhere to your firm's policies around gifts.

Key Insight

Many new developments are opening up enhanced possibilities for communicating with clients and building the business. Mobile technology can improve the frequency of contact, social media can expand your overall reach, and big data can provide insights about a person to enrich your conversations with them. Things are changing rapidly, so you'll need to keep abreast of what's coming to market. Of course, you need to be aware of regulations on this front as well.

MEET CHANGING DEMANDS

Russ Hill of Halbert Hargrove Global Advisors says it's a 24/7 world for both clients and employees these days, so you need to take steps to be responsive.

SAYS HILL:

There are trends at both the client level and the employee level that are driving new technology choices at our firm. With clients, more than ever it's twenty-four seven — they want to see information on their schedule, not when it's convenient for us. Mobile access for our advisors with a paperless office that lets them retrieve documents remotely helps meet client needs, as does our portal where we store documents and reports that clients can retrieve at any time.

> "Our technology team continues to monitor the landscape to see what new and relevant capabilities are emerging." RUSS HILL

Almost all employees at our firm are available twenty-four seven too. Because our staff is younger and doesn't follow an eight-to-five schedule, we have to provide some flexibility to make it easy for them to work remotely. For example, we try to have as much done on a laptop or a tablet as possible. That's just part of the deal these days if you want your staff to be fully engaged. All employees have a tablet and a mobile phone provided by the company, and we are trying out new laptops that have the portability of a tablet to see how they perform. We use mobile device management with blacklisting apps to support application compliance. This alerts our IT department when a blacklisted app is installed and helps us have more secure mobile policies.

We recently reconfigured our offices to an open bull pen environment, with low walls to enhance collaboration among staff members. We also have video capabilities in most of our conference rooms, which are used widely for interoffice meetings. In addition, all employees have a webcam so they can phone colleagues or clients and have a video conversation with them via their computer. We also answer the phones for all our locations from our corporate office using an Internet-based system that converts voice mail to email, because it's easier for our people to pick up messages that way.

We continually evaluate different technology options, given the rapid changes that are taking place. For example, we are testing devices for phones that support the archiving of text messages to meet retention requirements, plus a capability that will allow an administrator to deliver remote technical support to users. We are also interested in seeing what will happen with interactive games and simulations that will inevitably come to market to help increase the level of client engagement. There are lots of ways "gamification" can be used with financial plans, for example. Having checklists and progress bars can make things more interesting and help families become excited about reaching their goals.

It's vital to keep on top of new developments, but you also need to be thoughtful about any changes you make. Technology for technology's sake won't give you anything at all. To have a strong impact, your decisions on this front need to align with your business processes and the needs and demands of your clients and employees.

Key Insight

While technology has a definite impact on the client experience, it also affects the employee experience. Using technology to support how and where your staff works can improve satisfaction levels and help with both attracting and retaining talent. As more devices, mobile apps, and games come to market, see how they mesh with your strategy—and your firm's policies—and which ones make sense to adopt.

[3.2]

CONNECTING THE DOTS

ASSESS TECHNOLOGY DEVELOPMENTS

The RIA stories underscore the importance of adopting technologies that will support better communication and collaboration with clients. Mobile technology and social media may help on this front, as may new gadgets and applications coming to market. The sections that follow look at these three areas.

Mobile Technology

Mobile technology may provide a number of benefits, including:

- **Increased flexibility and productivity,** with a host of capabilities that can free you from an office environment and let you perform many functions immediately from virtually any location
- **Superior client service,** with quick response times to incoming requests that meet the demands of a world that operates 24/7
- **Better client collaboration,** with dynamic and interactive meetings that use touch-screen tablets for presentations
- **A secure environment,** with data in the cloud that can be reviewed without being downloaded to a device—valuable should a device be lost or stolen
- **The ability to attract clients and employees** among the younger generation of individuals who have grown up with smartphones and tablets at their fingertips

If you are looking to expand your mobile activities, consider the following:

- **Look at what's best suited for mobile** and don't try to do everything on a mobile device. In-depth research and rebalancing, for example, may be better suited to desktop applications.
- **Match technology options to different client needs,** such as videoconferencing sessions for younger clients who may not have the time or interest to meet in person.
- **Think about a mobile CRM platform** (if it's your hub) so you can access client, prospect, and partner data remotely.
- **Take steps to go paperless** to be able to retrieve documents efficiently and securely through mobile devices. You may want to evaluate available software programs that address computer and email security issues, and electronic file storage.
- **Look into electronic signature software** to eliminate the need to send documents through the mail or have clients physically come to your office to sign paperwork.
- **Protect your devices** with passwords in case they are lost or stolen, and look into mobile device management solutions to help secure and manage disparate devices.
- **Go mobile on your Web site** to provide an optimal viewing experience, regardless of which device is being used.

Social Media

As we have seen, social media can be a highly effective way of extending your reach. Of course, you need to be aware of any regulatory and/or reputational risk from using this medium. The SEC has issued guidance concerning its use by advisors, and suggests RIAs consider having policies and procedures specific to social media that address issues such as usage, content standards, frequency of monitoring, and approval for content. To support certain regulatory requirements, you may want to consider technology solutions that help automate the capture, retention, and supervision of social media communications.

If you are thinking about gearing up your social media activities, in addition to considering regulatory issues, review these five tips shared by BakerAvenue:

1. **Develop a plan.** You need to ask yourself what you can speak to with credibility that others want to hear; build your activities around this.
2. **Be deliberate and consistent about your communications.** If you have a schedule in place, your followers will know when to expect them. They can include blogs, tweets, emails, and items posted to your Web site.
3. **Appoint a community manager.** This person can have everything reviewed to make sure it meets your content and compliance standards.
4. **Get your entire organization on board.** Make sure everyone understands the plan and can be trained on what can be published—and where—so they can be involved.
5. **Do it right, or don't do it at all.** Poor execution can damage your brand, so determine whether you and the organization are really committed to the initiative before moving forward.

BakerAvenue produces original content, but it may also be possible to share content from other parties that you think will be of interest to your readers. Naturally, you'll need to investigate any intellectual property rights and obtain permission to post and distribute materials.

Also think about audience expectations, understand the nuances of each social media channel, and tailor your content accordingly. Be sure to consider the tone as well (personal versus professional), and length (small, "snackable" bits of information versus longer, blog-like posts) for each channel. Review social media in the context of your entire digital strategy, and understand the benefits it can create for search engine optimization so you can explore ways to promote your content across all digital channels.

New Gadgets and Applications

As we have shown, firms have started to adopt new devices and applications to improve "anywhere access" and to have more engaging client interactions. So where is all this headed? Fidelity believes that in just a few years, advisors can expect to work with wearable devices and use office products and even furniture that operate with cloud technology and integrated software platforms to help facilitate conversations with clients.

Technology will be less visible as computers disappear into user-friendly hardware like what's being showcased at Fidelity's prototype "office of the future." This office features more collaborative workspaces with lots of mobile and integrated technologies. These include a smart coffee table that lets clients sit in a relaxing setting with advisors while browsing the Web, sharing reports, and playing a game that teaches the basics of investing in an enjoyable and dynamic way. Looking forward, we should expect to see improved virtual desktops, video conferencing, and game mechanics.

As you look at these new developments, think about which ones mesh with your business and technology strategy and could have a positive impact on efficiency and the client experience. While many applications are first-generation versions at the moment, you may want to test some of them to see what they are capable of doing and how they might support your longer-term technology strategy.

Go to begreater.com to access additional resources supporting Chapter 3.

When you need to rely heavily on a range of technologies to run your front and back offices, it's essential to take the time to keep systems up to date, eliminate redundancies, and streamline activities as much as possible. But technology is about much more than operational efficiency today, and has the power to transform the way you work with clients. It plays a key role in how you position and differentiate your business, and it needs to be a central part of your growth strategy. This is especially true given the expectations of Gen X/Y clients and advisors, and the emergence of more tech-savvy competitors. Advisors need to embrace technology to work in a 24/7 world that, more and more, values collaboration and expects ready access to people and information.

In the next chapter, we look at how RIAs are taking steps to attract and retain the right type of clients for their firms.

[4]

Attracting and Retaining the Right Clients Propels Business Forward

97%

The percentage of high-performing firms* that carefully observe their ideal client profile to attract clients who are a good fit

*Firms in the top 25% of eligible survey respondents in the 2012 Fidelity RIA Benchmarking Study based on a composite ranking across three areas: AUM, earnings before owner's compensation, and revenue per full-time equivalent. Reference to the concept of "performing" in the name of this group isn't intended to connote investment returns, although that may be one of several identified factors that differentiate this group. The 2012 Fidelity RIA Benchmarking Study was conducted in collaboration with Quantuvis Consulting, Inc., an independent company not affiliated with Fidelity Investments. Respondents were RIA firms that custodied some portion of their assets with Fidelity Institutional Wealth Services (Fidelity). The study was conducted online from May 22, 2012, through July 30, 2012, and includes completed responses from 308 RIA firms. Fidelity was identified as the sponsor.

Clients

"No one ever became great by imitation." SAMUEL JOHNSON

RIAs have grown in size and sophistication, and there are many strong players in the field now. That's changed the game when it comes to attracting and retaining the right type of client for your firm. It may have become much more difficult to get your message out, find new prospects, and gather referrals. On top of this, as your clients grow older, you need to develop strong relationships with successive generations to help retain business over time. In this chapter, we look at three things we think you should consider to help stand apart from others and capitalize on business opportunities: (1) capture your points of differentiation, (2) identify your sweet spots and where you may be able to develop areas of expertise, and (3) stay visible with prospects, clients, and centers of influence, and connect in different ways.

Capture Your Points of Differentiation

Learn About

- Defining your points of differentiation
- Taking note of the competition
- The power of taglines
- Living your story

Given the level of competition in the market, you really need to consider why you are different so you can translate that into a distinctive story about your firm. That story should be powerful, yet simple, so all your staff members can rally around it and repeat it in a way that feels natural and comfortable. It's also important that the message comes through in a consistent fashion in all you do, including sales and marketing materials.

The stories that follow show what five RIAs have done on this front. The first three discuss crafting a message, and the last two highlight how that message can be reflected throughout your entire organization—from your brand to your office space to your people.

> "Everyone feels they have some competitive advantage, yet ninety-five percent of what we hear sounds the same." JERRY LUFF, CHIEF OPERATING OFFICER BAKERAVENUE

LIVE YOUR MANTRA

Greg Erwin and his colleagues at Sapient Private Wealth Management took deliberate steps to create points of differentiation for their firm and to have all employees describe these in the same way.

SAYS ERWIN:

Although our team had worked together for many years at a wirehouse, we hadn't clearly defined our value proposition. When we launched Sapient, we took the opportunity to create a persuasive story that reflects how we operate the business.

"You can't just say you are different; you really have to be different if you are to describe your firm in a compelling way." GREG ERWIN

Our mantra is "Win by not losing," and we knew we needed to adjust our way of investing if we were going to really deliver on that promise. So we introduced a much more specific approach to investment management, and recalibrated all our clients' portfolios.

Today, we absolutely know we are different because we took deliberate steps to make us so. We have coached our entire staff on how to express what we do. I now have a high degree of confidence that whenever anyone in our firm is asked why we are better than others, they'll have a good answer that will intrigue the person they are speaking with and encourage that person to learn more.

Key Insight

Many wealth advisory firms describe their capabilities in the same way. You have to take the time to really understand why you are different, and have your staff embrace your message so they can say it consistently and with passion.

DON'T FOLLOW THE PACK

Rick Buoncore of MAI Wealth Advisors saw that many firms were saying similar things in their marketing materials, and he wanted to approach his firm's message from a different angle.

SAYS BUONCORE:

Our story development started with us identifying three major firms that we admired and hoped we could be like one day. One of our investors did some mystery shopping for us and brought back the firms' marketing materials so we could evaluate how they were positioning themselves. We were surprised to see the similarities in what they said, and how they said it. Basically, they were all pounding their chest about who they were, what they did, and how long they had been in the business.

We couldn't compete with their history, so we took a different approach and decided to have our marketing materials be all about the client. The inside of our brochure has a picture of two people at the peak of a mountain and it says "Congratulations on your success." We go on to talk about how difficult the climb must have been, and the incredible leaps it must have taken to get there. We then tie this to an analogy about amassing wealth, and how we help our clients stay on top.

"In our early days, an investor in the firm said we really needed to create a brand that reflected who we are and what we stand for." RICK BUONCORE

This exercise helped us solidify who we are—and who we aren't. Our clients come to us wealthy; our job is to keep them wealthy. When someone says they want to beat the S&P 500® Index benchmark, for example, we say that's not our focus; it isn't our number-one aim. We want to understand our clients' overall financial aspirations and help them reach their larger goals.

Key Insight

It's useful to look at what the competition is saying in their marketing materials so that you can position your firm in a different way that captures the essence of who you are and what you do. Put yourself in your clients' shoes, and think what sentiments would appeal to them.

HAVE A TAGLINE WITH MEANING

John Waldron says wealth can introduce many complexities. He and his team at Waldron Wealth Management feel the best thing they can do for their clients is to try and make their lives as simple as possible, and this is reflected in the firm's tagline.

SAYS WALDRON:

Our clients are bombarded with so much information. As advice providers, we feel the biggest value we can provide is to simplify everything for our clients and present information in ways that help them easily make decisions to reduce their stress and anxiety. We have captured that in our firm's tagline—"Simplify life." It isn't just a catchy phrase, it's at the core of everything we do.

> "We feel it's the advice component, not the investment component, that's the driver of value for clients. So our message captures that." JOHN WALDRON

We have been using this message for more than twelve years now, and feel it's our main differentiator. Although it says what we do, we have hired a marketing and branding firm to help us tighten it up. In today's market, you really need to convey the passion you have for the business and what you believe in. We want to capture that in a stronger version of our message, make it consistent across everything we do, and develop a communications plan to support broader outreach.

Key Insight

A really good tagline can easily communicate the value that your firm delivers to clients, and is a succinct way to connect with your audience. As you create one, be sure it reflects what you do and how you describe the firm in other sales and marketing pieces.

CREATE A COMPLETE EXPERIENCE

Jerry Luff and the team at BakerAvenue want the firm's brand, culture, and story to connect with people looking for a more modern and personalized experience. As he puts it, "We aren't your father's investment firm."

SAYS LUFF:

Our CEO, Simon Baker, had the vision for how we should express who we are through everything we do — from our branding to the space we sit in to the people we hire. For example, we are located in the old Federal Reserve building in downtown San Francisco. The outside has massive columns and a very traditional, old-school feel. Inside, our space poses a juxtaposition. It's very creative, with exposed brick and lots of steel and glass, underscoring the fact that we have a solid foundation but are different from many traditional money managers.

"You have to do things differently today to stay ahead of the curve and in front of the competition." JERRY LUFF

We have also tried to reflect our culture on our Web site and in other marketing materials. The feel is friendly and dynamic. This includes showing members of our management team on the Web site with their business and "real me" looks, providing an instant connection to our true personalities. It's fun to see our director of client services with her hair in pigtails and a baseball cap on backwards, and our CEO playing with his dog. It's who we are and we want prospects to see the spirit and originality of our firm.

We also capture who we are and what we offer in our tagline—"Be different. Invest smart." We go against the conventional wisdom on Wall Street of staying fully invested regardless of the overall risk in the market. This approach to investing, and how we describe it, helps set our firm apart from others.

Key Insight

There are many aspects that influence how you are perceived by others—what you say, what you look like, and how you act can all have an impact. Be sure to walk the talk to reinforce the image you want people to take away.

CAPTURE YOUR BRAND IN ALL YOU DO

Sherri Daniels of Banyan Partners underscores the importance of having a strong brand and capturing what it represents visually in marketing materials. The firm has applied some consumer-oriented techniques for delineating different aspects of their product and service lineup.

SAYS DANIELS:

There is a culture that permeates everything we do at Banyan Partners, from our marketing materials to our physical location. When it comes to materials, for example, we have an in-house graphic design team that makes sure everything looks top-notch, because this is a key component that helps define the experience a client can expect when working with us.

> "Our CEO has a very aesthetic eye and we have been able to incorporate that throughout the organization in many ways." SHERRI DANIELS

From a branding standpoint, Peter Raimondi, our CEO, always talks of high-end car lines and credit cards as the branding standard, because they offer a series of options for different types of clients. The essence of each option is captured in their positioning and advertising. We have adopted a similar approach for our lines of business.

We have a main brand that offers customized portfolio management. Lotus and Vanda are complementary brands that utilize proprietary managed strategies. Our marketing team has looked at the target audience for each offering and the specific needs of the client base, and has built a look and feel for each brand that reflects these unique elements.

For our main brand, we use black in our sales and marketing materials to represent a high-end, tailored approach to client management, service, and investing. For Lotus and Vanda, which are named for highly evolved flowers known for their beauty and resilience, we have chosen other colors. This branding is another way we express who we are as a firm and the different aspects of what we provide. We take a lot of time to describe our complete range of capabilities to our centers of influence so they understand where we may be appropriate for different types of investors.

Key Insight

Consumer-oriented firms make it a priority to think about the end client and how to appeal to that client on an aesthetic and emotional level. Lessons can be learned from this that can be applied to how RIAs position and market different capabilities.

You don't have to be a larger firm like BakerAvenue or Banyan Partners to think about culture and image. Karen Keatley of Keatley Wealth Management—a firm with three people—designed her own office space. "I wanted a very specific look and hand-picked everything myself," she says. "It needed to be sleek without being overly modern, and feel comfortable without being pretentious or stuffy. It's a reflection of the personalities of our team members and the cheerful and solid relationships our clients can expect."

[4.1]

CONNECTING THE DOTS

CREATE A FIRM STORY

Firms often think their story is a simple elevator pitch — but it's much more than that. Your story is the embodiment of everything you do and is reflected in who you are, how you say it, and how you live it.

Ultimately, having a strong story with the supporting elements in place to back it up is essential to drive referrals from clients and centers of influence, and attract prospects. As you think about your story, consider four things:

1. It should be authentic:

- Choose words that capture who you really are. Consider taking steps to adjust your business model over time if the reality of who you are doesn't match the story and image you would like to project.

2. It should be different:

- Look at what others are saying to avoid falling into the trap of using the same words and expressions.
- Educate your staff on your key points of differentiation, and how your story should be described.
- Help your clients and centers of influence understand and articulate your value. It's easy to assume they are familiar with this, but you may miss out on referrals if that isn't the case.

3. It should be clear and easy to repeat:

- Simplicity can help all your stakeholders tell your story in a natural way, regardless of the venue or event.

4. It should be pulled through all visuals, materials, and more:

- Consistency will help reinforce your message. Be sure the same story is reflected across your brochures, Web site, and any other materials you use in the sales and client engagement process.
- Everything from your brand to your culture, location, and people says something about your firm. It's not a written story, elevator speech, or tagline that defines you — it's your personality, core values, and operating principles that are then expressed in these communication vehicles. Living it will help people see and feel who you are.

Case in Point—Crafting Your "About Us" Statement

You may be able to put together a narrative that's easy to repeat, but is it differentiated? Check out the About Us statement on most firms' Web sites. You'll see that in many cases the focus is on location, how big the firm is, and years in business, with a few additional comments about the offering. One need only ask the magic question, "So what?" to see there is typically very little to differentiate statements and demonstrate how clients will benefit from the relationship. Take the opportunity to be distinctive.

Ask the following questions:

- **Why:** Why do you do what you do? Refer to your strategic plan to look at your core purpose and why your firm exists.
- **Who:** Who do you serve best, and what are the challenges clients need your help to solve?
- **What:** What do you do to address their needs? What's different about your approach, investment philosophy, or business style?
- **How:** How do your clients benefit?

A Hypothetical Example: ABCD Advisory

ABCD Advisory was founded in 1987 by two former Peace Corps volunteers who wanted to start an investment firm with a focus on encouraging positive social change. The firm deals exclusively with family office solutions, particularly multigenerational solutions. Below are examples of the high-level response to each question:

- **Why:** To help individuals make significant social change in their communities
- **Who:** High-net-worth individuals who care about philanthropy
- **What:** We offer proprietary estate planning tools, an exclusive multigenerational focus, and a specialized team approach to service
- **How:** We help our clients spend their time, energy, and resources on positively impacting their communities

For illustrative purposes only.

These responses can now be used to craft a narrative that feels more differentiated than what we typically see.

About ABCD Advisory

(Why) Wealth can be used to make positive social change. As an RIA, we believe that when we protect and grow wealth for our clients, it enables them to make a significant impact on the world around them. **(Who)** ABCD Advisory specializes in the financial needs encountered by multigenerational, wealthy families who make philanthropy a priority in their lives. **(What)** Through proprietary estate planning tools, a specialized team approach to providing exceptional service, and an exclusive focus on multigenerational families, **(How)** we help our clients spend their time, energy, and resources on positively impacting their communities.

Thinking about these questions can help you begin to identify the key elements you'll want to capture in a concise paragraph that can help bring your story to life.

Go to begreater.com to access additional resources supporting Chapter 4.

Identify Your Sweet Spots

You can't be everything to everyone and do it well. Understanding the type of client who is best suited to your firm given your mission and competencies can help you bring on relationships you can manage effectively—and profitably.

Learn About

- Identifying your ideal client
- Strategies for attracting women
- Ways to reach Gen X/Y investors

The 2012 Fidelity RIA Benchmarking Study showed that many high-performing firms that had a clear understanding of their ideal client seemed to be better positioned to fulfill their clients' needs and provide a superior experience. While likely having a positive impact on retention and the flow of referrals, this clarity can also help with business development—seven out of 10 (72%) of these firms closed business within two prospect meetings or fewer, compared with 53% of all other eligible firms.*

Who you serve can help you differentiate your business by creating areas of expertise that meet those clients' needs. As you think about your ideal target clients given the strengths of your firm, also keep an eye on future opportunities with the wealth shifts that are under way. For example, women are projected to control a large portion of U.S. private wealth in the years to come, and Gen X/Ys may

> "You can't accept all comers, because not everyone will be a good fit for what you do best."
> JANE WILLIAMS, CHAIR AND CO-FOUNDER
> SAND HILL GLOBAL ADVISORS

*Eligible firms are participating firms that have two or more full-time employees, were established before 2008, and have more than $50 million in AUM.

SCREEN AND GROUP CLIENTS

After completing a merger, John Augenblick and the team at Rockwood Wealth Management stepped back and took a look at their client base to identify the distinct groups they were working with — and the ones they enjoyed the most.

SAYS AUGENBLICK:

When I was going through business school, I requested an internship at a local financial advisory firm to learn more about the industry. It was run by a sole proprietor who was a fee-only RIA who had left a wirehouse. I got an appreciation for how the business was being positioned, and joined full time in 2007.

"We are a smaller RIA, building the business one client at a time, so we want to get it right and ensure that we are a good fit for new clients, and vice versa." JOHN AUGENBLICK

In 2009, we merged with another smaller RIA. Like us, this firm was fee-only and doing comprehensive financial planning. They had a similar service model, portfolios, and technology. The pieces came together nicely and it made sense to join forces.

As we thought about our growth strategy, we decided we needed to examine our existing clients and get more focused on who we serve best. We began by bucketing them by profession and culture to see the distinct groups we were really working with. Then we asked who we liked working with and why, and why they value what we do for them. This resulted in identifying a small number of targets with very specific profiles. Looking forward, I see us divesting some clients who may not be a great fit for what we do, or who aren't a great fit personality-wise. After all, we want to work with people we enjoy and can really help.

Key Insight

You may be able to grow your business at a faster rate if you concentrate on your sweet spots, where you really add a lot of value to client relationships. Consider looking at your current roster of clients and creating profiles for different groups that are appropriate for your firm based on their needs and personalities. Use this to direct your client acquisition strategies moving forward.

CAPTURE TOMORROW'S OPPORTUNITIES TODAY

Adam Birenbaum felt the emerging wealthy segment was going unnoticed because many advisory firms try to attract high-net-worth clients. In response, Buckingham Asset Management created new areas of expertise for its younger staff members to serve these investors who may be tomorrow's millionaires.

SAYS BIRENBAUM:

I believe that younger clients want advisors who are talented, but who they can work closely with through their investing life. As a result, we are really focused on bringing our younger advisors up to speed as quickly and as prudently as possible, and providing opportunities for them to team with investors of a similar age.

We have created areas of expertise where these advisors can work with new lawyers, doctors, and other professionals who are just getting established in their own business—many of whom, I believe, are being overlooked by RIAs. What better place to find your next-generation client than with these individuals who need advice now as they are just launching their careers? In addition, what a great teaching ground this provides for younger advisors who don't necessarily have the networks at this stage to develop relationships with high-net-worth prospects.

"Many advisory firms are trying to go upscale. That means some folks who are going to be great future clients are going unnoticed. We wanted to begin nurturing these relationships today." ADAM BIRENBAUM

The initiative is in an early growth phase, but we are excited about the potential it represents as we look to develop strong relationships that will enable us to support tomorrow's wealthy.

Key Insight

Over the coming years, a great deal of money will pass from boomers to the Gen X/Y segment. Clearly, this is a group that RIAs should be nurturing. Think about the unique needs and preferences of these younger investors, and provide opportunities for them to work with advisors who will support them over the years.

[4.2]

CONNECTING THE DOTS

IDENTIFY YOUR IDEAL CLIENT GROUPS

Most RIAs aren't large enough to serve a lot of different types of clients with different needs. As we have seen from these stories, it's helpful to know who your target clients should be and then align your business accordingly. As Jane Williams of Sand Hill Global Advisors points out, "going a mile deep versus a mile wide" can help create a level of expertise and a good reputation in a particular area, aiding business development. It's also useful to think about how the profile of attractive investors will change over time given the wealth shifts we mentioned. This includes monies flowing to women and Gen X/Y investors.

As you begin to think about your ideal clients, it can be helpful to describe the attributes of your best clients today. This exercise might include the following:

ATTRIBUTE	DESCRIPTION
Financial profile	Annual income, investable assets, net worth
Personal and family profile	Age, marital status, family composition, generational opportunities
Educational and professional background	Degrees, alma mater, industry, profession
Life stage	Preretiree, retiree, peak earning years
Top three life goals	What they want to achieve in life
Interests and causes they care about	Hobbies, leisure activities, charitable causes
Most important financial issues in their lives	What keeps them up at night
Top three ways you help them	How you help them achieve their life goals and address their pressing financial issues

For illustrative purposes only.

These attributes can help you create profiles of a number of distinct groups you feel you can serve well. For example:

PROFILE 1
This ideal client group is: • Approximately 45 years old with a master's degree or PhD • Typically male, working long hours in the health care profession • Earning an annual salary of $250,000+, with a net worth of $1.5 million+ • Raising several children and concerned about the cost of college education • Looking to our firm for financial planning, investment management, and college savings advice

For illustrative purposes only.

As you consider ideal client groups, be sure to evaluate potential new groups you could be serving.

POTENTIAL NEW GROUPS	HOW YOUR FIRM COULD ADD VALUE
	What makes you qualified to serve this group? What distinctive products and services could you provide? How will this impact who you serve today? What synergies exist with those you serve today?
Younger clients	
Women	
Children of existing clients	
Executives	
Others	

With this information in hand, you can begin to think about your strengths relative to the competition, and why individuals who fall into these categories should consider working with you.

Working with Women

For advisors looking to unlock growth for the future, women may offer an interesting, yet often overlooked, opportunity. They represent a significant demographic shift that may affect the makeup of a financial advisor's client base. This is particularly significant when considering your heterosexual clients. With women outliving men by five to six years on average,* there is a good chance that in the case of a married couple, the wife will one day become the remaining client. If you aren't engaging women now, the relationship may not be as strong as you need it to be. Here are a number of actions to consider:

- **Make participation by both spouses a requirement.** Institute a policy whereby both members of the couple are encouraged to attend meetings.

- **Host group events.** Arrange interesting events to get to know the wives better.

- **Listen to both spouses' concerns through ongoing dialogue and planning.** Hear and understand the wife's concerns to help her open up and share her financial hopes and fears.

- **Deliver ongoing financial education.** Provide educational events and materials to help female clients find their voice in financial discussions.

- **Organize the family's critical financial documents.** Pull together important information in one location to make it easier for a surviving spouse to deal with an extremely difficult time of life.

- **Show your appreciation.** Routinely express thanks for the wife's continued trust—a simple gesture that can make a big difference.

*"Why Women Live Longer," Thomas Kirkwood, *Scientific American,* October 2010.

Working with Younger Investors

If you are looking to work with the Gen X/Y segment, here are a few generalities to keep in mind:

- **Consider skipping extensive talk about who you are.** Before they meet you, these young adults have likely looked you up online and read your background, so be sure to manage your brand online and keep introductions to a minimum.

- **Keep your message factual and detailed.** Tell them how you run your business and plan to manage their affairs.

- **Be prepared and patient with the questions they may ask.** They have witnessed or heard about many financial scandals, so you'll need to build trust.

- **Demonstrate the value you'll provide for the fees you'll charge.** Know they are exceptionally price conscious and will want to understand the extent of the relationship.

- **Show a flexible communication style.** They'll likely be tech savvy and used to communicating how and when they like.

- **Recognize they are often too busy to focus and take the next step.** Send them periodic articles or links to blogs or tweets to show your continued interest.

- **If they do become a client, up the fun factor.** Be sensitive to their life stage and interests.

Go to begreater.com to access additional resources supporting Chapter 4.

Stay Visible and Connect in Different Ways

Naturally, as competition heats up, more advisors are going after the same investor. It's much harder today to sit back and hope business comes your way because you are doing a good job. Whether you are looking for referrals from clients or centers of influence, or business from new prospects, you have to work at attracting and retaining relationships in a differentiated and diligent way.

Learn About

- Connecting with clients on an emotional level
- The use of social media
- Tactics for increasing your close rate
- Building business with the next generation

Being front and center with clients and prospects and deliberate in how you engage with them can help you win new business and turn your clients into promoters of the firm. The following stories show how seven RIAs are reaching out to build their brand and their business.

"To attract more business, you need to tell your story from a higher mountain top."

KELLY TREVETHAN, REGIONAL MANAGING DIRECTOR
UNITED CAPITAL FINANCIAL ADVISERS

SPEAK TO INVESTORS' CONCERNS

Kelly Trevethan says understanding how people feel about money from an emotional perspective can help you identify the best investment strategies and estate plans to address their concerns. United Capital Financial Advisers has taken this approach to a new level.

SAYS TREVETHAN:

We are all hard-wired to some extent, based on our childhood experiences and how we saw our parents handle financial issues. United Capital has developed exclusive tools that help us get to the root of that, and build appropriate wealth and estate plans that reflect each client's concerns. If a person is fear-based, for example, we need to use strategies that have lower risk and less volatility so we can keep that client on track to achieve his or her goals. The tools have received a lot of publicity and really get everyone engaged.

> "United Capital has worked with psychologists and behavioral finance experts to develop tools that help us understand how our clients feel about money on an emotional level." KELLY TREVETHAN

We have also utilized these behavioral techniques in a direct marketing program that asks a series of targeted questions formulated to get people excited about meeting with us for a second opinion about what they are doing. We mail to about five thousand households every month and get anywhere from six to twelve appointments with qualified prospects.

This program has generated substantial new business, and I feel two things have contributed to its success. First, the invitations are designed to attract individuals who are concerned about their money, and show we can help people manage their wealth if we were to go through another significant downturn. Second, they are aimed at individuals who are at a point in their life when they are likely to be second-guessing what they are doing. So we get a lot of responses from people who are about to retire, or have just retired.

We also look to centers of influence to grow the business, and feel the best way to maximize a relationship is to have them experience what it's like to work with our firm. It's like inviting them to your restaurant for a meal so they can taste the quality of your food firsthand. We meet with attorneys and other professionals and go into detail about how we engage with our clients so they can understand, and appreciate, our approach. Ongoing communication is also very important and it has to be personal — it can't just be having a phone call or sending an email. We like to augment this with unexpected touches. For example, we send the CPAs we work with something fun during tax time — like a survival kit. A gift basket with Starbucks® coffee and a case of Red Bull® always gets a little chuckle.

Key Insight

Depending on a person's past experiences, he or she may prefer one type of financial solution over another. Think about how clients feel about money from an emotional perspective, so you can customize solutions they'll really value to help them grow and preserve their wealth.

EDUCATE CLIENTS AND PARTNERS

Sherri Daniels had been running an investment management firm that was very marketing oriented before joining Banyan Partners. She has seen successful targeted campaigns and is beginning to introduce similar tactics at Banyan.

SAYS DANIELS:

We have been working on a lot of acquisitions over the past few years and on the integration of these firms, so we have been continually creating new collateral to go with our expanded investment offerings and services. We are now at a point where we are taking steps to introduce targeted campaigns to educate our clients and partners on the different investment strategies we provide. Past experience has shown me this can be a very successful way to develop new business.

Key Insight

Technology plays a central role in our lives today, and social media can help round out your marketing initiatives. Naturally, it's just one piece of the puzzle and needs to align with your other activities—all of which need regular attention and follow-through to have an impact.

DEMONSTRATE YOUR VALUE PROPOSITION

Richard Burridge says his team at RMB Capital invests many hours getting to know prospects. This builds trust from the outset and helps both parties determine whether there will be a good fit.

SAYS BURRIDGE:

We have a high-touch approach that helps our advisors form a deep personal connection with prospects and clients, which tends to attract and retain relationships that are right for the firm. Before someone decides to hire us, we typically invest between twenty and forty hours in the "getting to know each other" phase. Our view is that we can't give any advice until we have gathered all the information needed to completely understand their circumstances. So we ask for copies of their tax returns, estate planning documents, life insurance policies, investment accounts, and so on.

> "If a prospect is willing to hand over many personal documents before he or she has hired you, there has been a leap of faith that demonstrates trust." RICHARD BURRIDGE

A team of advisors assesses everything, and we present our observations in a two- to three-hour meeting. This includes a first draft of what the relationship would look like in terms of investment allocation and various planning recommendations. Since we have done all this work up front, it helps prospects understand our value proposition. This approach also helps us determine whether prospects are a good fit for us—if they appreciate what we do and if their investment philosophy syncs up with our approach.

Key Insight

Prospecting can take a lot of time, so you need to have a high success rate when it comes to turning leads into clients. Making an up-front investment during initial discussions can help create a sense of trust, show what your firm is all about, and close business that's suited to your approach.

SPREAD KNOWLEDGE

Adam Birenbaum says a team of national thought leaders at Buckingham Asset Management helps keep the firm front and center in the press. Additionally, ongoing prospect and client events have created a group of advocates who spread the firm's message to friends and colleagues.

SAYS BIRENBAUM:

One of the different things we have done at Buckingham is to create an entire team of national thought leaders. Our directors of research, investment strategy, personal finance, investor education, and investor advocacy are all writers and bloggers featured in major news media. They have a gigantic following and serve as educational pillars to our investors and our advisors.

"When you don't have the advertising budget of the large Wall Street firms, you have to find creative ways to get publicity." ADAM BIRENBAUM

We are big on sharing deep institutional knowledge throughout our community to help our investors be knowledgeable. We want them to understand our process, what we are aiming to do for them, and why. To reinforce this message, our communications strategy uses a combination of social media, webinars, and traditional print. We augment this with a large number of regular prospect and client events.

At the end of the day, I think firms that strive to be greater have done a tremendous job of turning their clients into advocates—their business development arsenal. We find that people who come to our events end up following us on social media and being our marketing apostles. They are the ones telling their friends and colleagues about our business.

Key Insight

Outreach via social media,* webinars, traditional print, and client and prospect events all play a role in creating market awareness for your firm. Committed and loyal clients can also help spread the word about your products and services, so consider steps to turn them into an additional source of information about your capabilities.

REACH THE NEXT GENERATION

John Waldron says his firm takes well-thought-out steps to engage its clients' children and teach them useful lessons about managing the wealth they'll ultimately be inheriting.

SAYS WALDRON:

Because we have a family office, our advice is also about multigenerational planning and decisions around transferring wealth. We need to have a deep-rooted understanding of the family to do that, which includes knowing the matriarch and patriarch, plus the second and third generations. To connect with the younger people, we have implemented a generational education program, which we think is a big differentiator for us.

"We absolutely expect to continue being the advisor for a family over the years, because we engage the next generation actively and intensely." JOHN WALDRON

*Be knowledgeable about regulations regarding social media and your firm's specific policies.

One of the greatest concerns for our clients is whether their children will be equipped to deal with the wealth they'll inherit, and how they'll deal with it emotionally and socially. Since most of our clients didn't grow up with money, they don't know what to expect. We offer a well-rounded educational curriculum for their children.

Fact-based topics touch on what happens when money transfers from one generation to another, the purpose of a trust, the role of a trustee, and budgeting. Other issues touch on the pros and cons of having money, why people may want to be your friend, and the importance of creating a prenuptial agreement if you are planning to get married. It's amazing some of the dialogue this generates. There is a definite interest in discussing issues that often aren't touched upon at a family level, and doing so with trusted advisors where the emotion has been taken out of the equation.

Key Insight

Significant monies will be changing hands in the years to come as wealth is transferred from one generation to another. If you are dealing with a high-net-worth client base, consider ways to reach out to your clients' children to start—or strengthen—a relationship with them to put you in good shape to remain the advisor for the family over the long term.

BE SELECTIVE IN WHAT YOU DO

Greg Erwin says marketing and business development aren't natural functions for many advisory firms. This was the Achilles' heel for Sapient Private Wealth Management, too, before the team put in place a plan it felt comfortable with, and will follow through on.

SAYS ERWIN:

Marketing and business development were our biggest weaknesses, as they are for many RIAs, so we have spent the last couple of years putting in place a strategy that works for us culturally. I think you need to keep things simple. Although savvy marketing people can suggest a wide range of tactics to build the business, in reality there may be two things out of ten that make sense for you. We ferreted out a few ideas that we liked and were willing to do consistently, and that's what we focus on.

While we don't view community outreach as a business development strategy, it has helped raise our firm's profile. Like anything in life, if you go into something with truly authentic intentions, unexpectedly good things can come your way. Our involvement encompasses a wide range of areas, including track and field, which is my passion. Through the efforts of a lot of people, we were able to participate in bringing back the Olympic track and field trials to our city in 2008 and 2012, and our city will host them again in 2016. It's an odyssey that was started in 2005 with Nike to make Oregon the center of the track and field universe, and to resurrect a sport that people have been losing interest in for a couple of decades now. We feel community involvement like this is very important, and we encourage all our employees to be active in some fashion.

"We were fortunate to have brought in enough referrals over the years to grow at a satisfactory pace. The landscape has changed today—some of our biggest competitors didn't even exist before." GREG ERWIN

Key Insight

Not everyone feels comfortable doing marketing and business development, so you need to find the types of initiatives that suit who you are so you can carry them out in a way that's natural and authentic. Getting involved with community ventures that you really care about can also help you build a network of contacts.

[4.3]

CONNECTING THE DOTS

BUILD BUSINESS

The RIA stories suggest a number of important steps to help attract and retain the right type of clients for your firm.

- **Create market awareness**
  - Uncover ways to be easily found so people can reach out to you
  - Consider targeted mail campaigns
  - Focus on thought leadership and using the Web, social media, and other avenues to get the word out about your point of view

- **Build rapport**
  - Tailor your message and marketing materials so they resonate with your target prospects
  - Address how clients feel about money on an emotional level
  - Find ways to have prospects experience what it may feel like to be a client of your firm

- **Maintain an ongoing connection with clients**
  - Provide ongoing education through webinars, social media, and in-person events
  - Involve your staff in causes that are meaningful to the broader community
  - Reach the next generation of investors and give them a jump on financial issues by developing communications and education programs

The "Three Cs" to Deepening Client Engagement

At the root of many of the strategies RIAs have discussed is gaining a deeper understanding of the clients being served. We often ask advisors: How well do you know your clients? Do you capture family and occupational updates and recreational interests to drive follow-up discussions and communications? Does your CRM system allow this information to be recorded and shared throughout your organization?

To support this, we developed a disciplined approach to getting to know your clients, called the "Three Cs." It's designed to help you collect information, capture it in an easily accessible place, and capitalize on what you have learned.

1. Collect

It's helpful to gather a variety of information about your prospects, clients, and centers of influence. This means asking basic business questions around financial goals, risk tolerance, and investment preferences, and then moving beyond this to identify key areas in their personal lives. Consider collecting the following information:

- What they are passionate about
- Where they went to school and why they selected that school
- Their hobbies and, if they have children, their children's hobbies
- Priorities for their children beyond financial stability
- Names and birthdays of every member of their immediate family
- Philanthropic and volunteer interests or goals
- Favorite foods, flowers, and vacation destinations
- Preferred communication style, including texting, email, postal delivery, or calls to their office or home

2. Capture

Even when there is a close personal connection, details may not be captured in a CRM system. Yet clients want to feel known by everyone when they call. If you record what you learn and share it with others on your team, anyone can assist your clients and make them feel comfortable.

As you compile information about a client's interests, you may also begin to see themes. Just as many companies gather information on what we buy, when we buy it, and what form of payment we use, you can collect useful details to strengthen your relationships. So don't just ask—be sure to capture, too.

3. Capitalize

Once you have collected and captured information, you need to put it to work. After all, it's meaningless unless you capitalize on it. Let's look at an example.

You collect information: One of your clients has a child who has chosen to attend Dartmouth. After digging deeper, you learn the family has always vacationed in New Hampshire, so the state holds particular meaning for the child.

You capture information: You record the family's personal interests along with the college selection information in your CRM system for later use.

You capitalize on information: At the start of the school year, you research and recommend a few nearby shops and restaurants in the area. You also send your client a gift certificate for a B&B close to the campus, with a note wishing the family well as they embark on a new adventure in an extra-special place.

There are other ways to capitalize on information. For example:

- Find books, articles, or gifts that align with client interests, while keeping in mind your firm's policies on gifting.
- Connect your clients with people who share mutual interests.
- Send handwritten follow-up notes that relate to something you discussed.

On a broader note, you should try to identify themes in your pool of clients and prospects. For example:

- Do they share hobbies, interests, and backgrounds?
- Are there consistencies in the types of things they care about?
- Are there similarities in professional or academic backgrounds, charitable endeavors, hobbies, or travel interests?

You can use this information to plan seminars, workshops, dinners, and sports outings for like-minded people. You can also use this to inform topic areas for educational forums, newsletter articles, or content for your Web site. For instance, if many of your clients are concerned about raising financially responsible children, you could host a speaker series on this topic. This information could also make its way to your Web site for your clients' future reference.

Go to begreater.com to access additional resources supporting Chapter 4.

Differentiation is key to attracting and retaining clients in a market where RIAs are becoming larger and more savvy. You'll need to take the time to understand where you excel compared with the competition to be able to effectively describe your relative strengths to your target clients and business partners. Creating areas of expertise, expressing a story that's reflected in everything you do, and actively engaging clients and prospects in different ways using a range of media can help with your growth strategies.

While attracting and retaining clients is important, attracting and retaining highly qualified employees is equally important. In the next chapter, we look at the staffing side of the equation, and hear stories about how firms have taken steps to identify, develop, and engage top talent.

[5]

Hiring and Developing Top Talent Supports Growth

57.5%

The average total compensation to total revenue ratio*

*The 2014 Fidelity RIA Benchmarking Study was conducted between May 6 and June 30, 2014, in collaboration with an independent third-party research firm unaffiliated with Fidelity Investments. The experiences of the RIAs who responded to the study may not be representative of the experiences of other RIAs and aren't an indication of future success. A total of 411 firms completed the study.

Teams

"Teamwork is the ability to work together toward a commo vision—the ability to direct individual accomplishment toward organizational objectives. It's the fuel that allows common people to attain uncommon results." ANDREW CARNEGI

As we spoke with the RIAs featured in this book about business models, planning, technology, and client engagement, they all acknowledged that, in the end, a firm's success rests with its people. It's their knowledge, skills, and attitudes that will bring these areas to life and determine how well each of them is handled. Whether you are hiring for succession or for building your firm's infrastructure and promoting growth, highly motivated staff members striving to do their best can help evolve your firm, execute a strategic plan, harness technologies, and enhance the client experience. This underscores the importance of being thoughtful about each and every new hire you make, and continually investing in developing and engaging your people to retain top talent. As you do this, you naturally need to keep your firm's mission front and center at all times, and align your team against your strategy. In this chapter, we discuss how to (1) identify the right new hires for your firm, (2) develop employees through personal growth plans and regular feedback, and (3) engage employees by providing both financial and nonfinancial rewards.

Identify the Right New Hires for Your Firm

Learn About

- Necessary attributes
- Finding candidates
- Describing your culture
- Using interns
- The importance of diversity

Every new hire, no matter how long he or she stays with your firm, will have an impact on your business, so it's critical that you take the time to make the best employment decisions. Of course, you need to start with a bigger picture of what your organizational structure looks like, where you have gaps, and the positions you need to fill. With this in mind, you can define the requirements of different jobs, how teams and reporting structures work, what it's going to take for someone to be successful in each role, and where you might find the best candidates. It's also important to recognize that talented individuals will likely be considering multiple options. Just as you need a compelling story that describes your differentiators to attract and retain clients, you need one to attract and retain employees, too.

The stories that follow show how six RIAs identify potential candidates and take steps to ensure that expectations are set appropriately about the firm's culture, work environment, and career opportunities.

"We can't have any mediocre people on staff—even one would really dispirit the others who are working so hard." JOHN AUGENBLICK, PRESIDENT
ROCKWOOD WEALTH MANAGEMENT

TEST SKILLS AND PERSONALITY

Jerry Luff says it's clearly important for a potential new staff member to have the right set of skills and experience for a particular job. After that, however, the candidate needs to mesh with the firm's culture at BakerAvenue to be considered for a position.

SAYS LUFF:

When we are contemplating a new addition to our staff, there are specific requirements that a person needs to meet, including having the right attitude to fit in with our team. We are a tight-knit group of just over twenty people, and feel we have a very special culture. We can't afford to have someone come in and alter that and make the environment challenging.

We have been lucky in that many candidates have been referred to us by people who know our firm well and have come across someone they think will be a great fit. That has eliminated the need to do a lot of active recruiting, and it has also provided us with candidates who have been vetted somewhat already — especially from a personality perspective.

"We are looking for very specific attributes in a new hire. Above all, he or she needs to have good chemistry with the team." JERRY LUFF

We start discussions with candidates by reviewing our needs and the skills they have to do the job well. Once we feel there is alignment on that front, we have them come to our corporate office to meet everyone. To test the chemistry, we like to have them be part of a team-building event, which is something we do fairly regularly. For example, we had a person join us at an off-site in Sonoma for a few days, where we were reviewing our strategic initiatives. It provided an opportunity for him to experience how we work together and enjoy each other's company. It also let us see how he interacted with everyone in a range of settings. You can learn so much more in this type of situation than in a traditional in-office interview — and it shows we aren't traditional, which is part of our key message to the market.

Key Insight

You need to have a very clear idea about the traits you are looking for in an individual, and the type of person who will work well with your team. Someone may be extremely qualified for a position from a skill and experience perspective, but may not have the personality you need. Consider meeting candidates in different settings to see how they act.

LEVERAGE OUTSIDE PROFESSIONALS AND PREPARE JOB DESCRIPTIONS

At LourdMurray, Blaine Lourd looks to hire self-starters who enjoy a lot of autonomy. His firm uses outside search professionals to fill many positions, and provides them with detailed job descriptions to help screen candidates.

SAYS LOURD:

We want to have a motivated and ambitious staff, and build a culture where people feel free to stretch their intellectual capacity and reach all their goals. When we are looking to fill positions in areas like operations, technology, and client service, we use outside search professionals to help us identify the right people. I may even consider doing this for advisors at some point, although, to date, these have been individuals we have met in the market. While we need to pay for these external services, I think tapping into skilled resources can be very helpful. I don't have the time or the expertise to post jobs and sift through resumes, and neither does anyone else in the firm.

"We have been very pleased with the caliber of individuals that outside search professionals have been able to find for us." BLAINE LOURD

Before we reach out for assistance, we create a job description that helps us articulate the skills we are looking for, and the type of person who will work well in our company. We discuss this with the outside search professionals so they understand our requirements and can zero in on the most appropriate people for us to meet. Of course, once you work with professionals several times, they get to know the dynamics of your firm, which helps them with the screening process.

Key Insight

In filling certain positions, outside search professionals may be a good choice, as they can devote the time needed to find and vet candidates. Detailed job descriptions can help them better understand the critical skill sets and attributes you are looking for to make any search as productive as possible.

USE A RANGE OF RECRUITING TACTICS

Richard Burridge says RMB Capital uses a number of different approaches to finding good candidates. These include hiring interns, tapping into professional and personal networks, and utilizing outside recruiters and social media sites.

SAYS BURRIDGE:

We have hardworking people who always put the clients' needs ahead of everything else. It's important that potential employees understand and relate to this "client first" culture, which supports retention as well as growth. After all, when clients like and trust you, they are more likely to make referrals.

"We invest a lot of time trying to find the right people for our firm, and we reach out in a number of ways." RICHARD BURRIDGE

We tend to use a number of different approaches to grow our team. For example, we have a formal recruiting program in place that includes building relationships with several universities. We participate in internships and career fairs, and we actively engage with the schools' career centers throughout the year to stay top of mind with the faculty, staff, and students. This has been very successful for us, paving the way for conversations with some of the best candidates. We hire several interns each summer so they can get a better understanding of what it's like to have a career in our industry and what it's like to work at RMB. Some of our past interns have been offered full-time positions after graduation, which is a win-win situation because we have already developed a level of familiarity and confidence in one another.

Given our growth, there has also been a need to hire seasoned people who can fill other mid- or senior-level positions in the firm. In such cases, we tend to rely on our professional and personal networks, as well as executive recruiters. Potential new non-entry-level hires typically have interviews with about ten people across the firm, so we can get a good perspective on their strengths and overall fit.

Our firm also has a page on LinkedIn®, and we post open positions there and provide a link to the page in the careers section of our Web site. Social media sites can play a useful role in recruiting, given their wide reach.

Key Insight

Consider developing ties with a number of universities to put you in touch with new graduates and students looking for internships, and adding social media to your recruiting strategies. Your professional and personal contacts may be a good source for individuals looking for a more senior-level position in the firm.

ADD INTERNS TO THE MIX AND VET CANDIDATES WELL

Russ Hill says the staff at Halbert Hargrove Global Advisors understands the need for everyone to pull in the same direction if the firm is to be successful. The team is actively engaged in interviewing any potential new hire to make sure there is a good fit.

SAYS HILL:

We have a very collaborative environment here. When I knew I was going to share a story about our people, I asked employees for their thoughts. They spoke about the strong culture we have in the office, and how it's a very comfortable environment where there is a lot of trust. They also mentioned the regular reviews and encouragement they receive, and how all this makes them want to work really hard.

When we describe our firm to candidates, we capture many of the sentiments our employees expressed to me. We say we have a cooperative, family-oriented firm that values lifelong learning, uncompromising ethics, and putting the clients' interests first. You might hear some of these words elsewhere in the marketplace, but our employees truly believe them and can point to many examples of things we have done that reinforce our core values.

> "Our staff doesn't want to have any weak links that could affect their ability to succeed." RUSS HILL

We tend to use a lot of interns, which provides a good opportunity to evaluate their skill set and personality before making a hiring decision. We are fortunate that the largest university system in the state is headquartered in our city, and their largest campus is here too. When we put out a notice for an intern, we typically get about fifty applicants. In part, this is because previous interns tell their friends about our firm — something we work hard to promote.

We have gone from an "accidental" to an "on purpose" intern program, and try to make the experience a good one all around. We have someone who manages the program, and any staff member who wants to use an intern must go to this person and describe his or her project, which then gets prioritized. The interns are given real work, which may include doing financial plans, helping on service teams, or using our software systems for analytics.

I think it's good to have several interns on board at the same time, as they can support each other and jointly ask for additional help in a particular area, or express the desire to learn more. We also want them with our firm year-round, even if it's just a few hours a week. That way, they won't forget what they have learned and can appreciate the direction we are taking — how we are innovating and changing. This helps them decide if they like financial and wealth counseling and want to pursue it as a career.

When we are ready to fill full-time positions, we use an outside firm to do background checks, plus the tools that another firm provides to help assess personality, attitudes, and values. Each candidate then goes through a rigorous interview process that includes all the staff in our head office. These candidates may be interviewed by five or so people at one time, and have to make the case as to why they should be hired. We don't assign questions to the interviewers, but let them do their own thing. While there may be some repetition, it can be very revealing to see how a candidate responds depending on who is asking the question.

Our associates are very nice, but they also want to work with people who can carry their own load. Not everybody makes it through the interview process — even some of the interns we thought were really good. It comes down to work ethic. Our staff knows that their future depends in part on how well a new hire performs, so they are very engaged in the interviews, and dig deep to ensure that we make offers to the best people who are willing to work hard.

Even though we have a family feeling, we are really more like a sports team on which each person is a coach, leader, and team member simultaneously, and we want — require, really — the best possible player at every position. At our firm, adequate performance is rewarded with a generous severance package. While it's not easy or pleasant, even with formal reviews and development plans in place, some hires may not work out.

Key Insight

If you are going to use interns, give them real work that lets them experience the profession and decide whether this is the right career to pursue. Also, consider having them work throughout the year, even for a few hours each week, so they stay connected and can see your strategy in motion. Remember, not all people work out, even with conscientious hiring and sound development plans. If this is the case, take action to handle the situation in a respectful and timely manner. It isn't good for the individual or the firm otherwise.

CONSIDER DIVERSITY

RIAs need to develop an employee base that represents a mix of genders, ages, and ethnicities given the changes we are seeing in the marketplace. Michael Nathanson at The Colony Group recognizes this, and has been taking steps to broaden the firm's talent pool.

SAYS NATHANSON:

You need to hire the right people, and also the right mix of people. For example, wealth is increasingly being created and/or managed by women, and we need to have gender diversity in our ranks to support that trend. Women represent over one-third of our staff today, and we have a good gender mix at the senior level and in our ownership base, unlike many well-established firms that still tend to be male dominated.

While I think it would be an inaccurate generalization to say women like working with female advisors, I think we can assume that at least some women like to work with a person who might be more sensitive to gender-specific issues. It stands to reason that firms that want to attract female clients now and in the future should make sure they are adequately staffed with women at all organizational levels. They should also adopt philosophies and policies that prospective employees will see as accommodating women, such as providing the flexibility to balance work and family responsibilities.

> "We are always looking for the best talent, and we understand that we should promote diversity throughout the firm." MICHAEL NATHANSON

Beyond gender, we think that having a diverse staff in terms of age enriches the firm by providing different points of view and ways of looking at the world. It also makes us more attractive to the next generation. We have taken steps to bring on younger advisors, and many of our partners are under forty years of age. We'll continue to do more on the diversity front to build a strong team that represents the demographic shifts we are witnessing.

Key Insight

Wealth is beginning to shift to different segments of the population. Gender, age, and ethnic diversity among your base of professionals can help round out your thinking and make your firm more attractive to tomorrow's high-net-worth investors.

[5.1]

CONNECTING THE DOTS

FIND THE BEST CANDIDATES

As we have seen from these stories, there are a number of ways to find qualified candidates for positions you are looking to fill, including engaging universities for new graduates and interns, tapping into personal and professional networks, and using outside recruiters and social media sites.

If you are looking to engage universities, Dr. Charles Chaffin, Director of Academic Programs and Initiatives at the Certified Financial Planner Board of Standards, Inc. (CFP Board), says you need to be creative. It isn't enough be a guest lecturer anymore. You need to reach out in a number of ways to build awareness and foster a good relationship. This might include becoming part of an advisory board or providing resources and financial support for a program. In addition, both faculty and students are asking more about the career path that's available. You should also outline the experiences they can expect, and the type of training and mentorship that will be provided.

Before you start looking for good candidates, you should have a job description in hand that summarizes the roles and responsibilities for each open position to help improve your chances of identifying people with the right skills, experience, behaviors, and personality.

As you create job descriptions, it can be helpful to think about what has worked well for you in the past and why some individuals have succeeded where others have failed. Did people who prospered have certain traits you should be focusing on? As you hire, also think about the capabilities you may need as your firm evolves. Describe what your firm might look like one to five years from now, and what this means for the type of work you'll be doing and the talent you'll need.

Develop Rewarding Internships

Active internship programs can help you tap into a new generation of talent and determine how well individuals work with your team before hiring for a full-time position. To successfully recruit from universities, you'll need a plan of action. This should include a list of schools you'll approach, a story that will connect with the executive directors, faculty, and students, and how you plan to nurture each relationship so it becomes highly fruitful over time.

Be aware that interns may have higher expectations today than they did in the past. You need to take the time to craft meaningful learning opportunities so they consider working with your firm once they graduate and report a favorable experience to their school and to other students.

Here are a few things to keep in mind:

- Many of today's financial planning interns come with solid credentials, technological know-how, and social media skills that may benefit your organization. Make the most of them.
- Interns want meaningful work that teaches them something new or enables them to further develop their "soft skills." This might include interacting with clients and staff and learning some of the nuances of the financial planning profession. Of course, be sure to underscore the importance of client confidentiality and boundaries regarding what should and shouldn't be discussed.
- One of the industry's greatest assets is the diversity of roles that are available, from analysis to technology to marketing to administration. Interns are often assessing which area of the business has the most appeal. Let them experience different aspects of your firm so they can test things out.
- Be clear about the work your interns will perform to eliminate any ambiguity and help them make a useful contribution.
- Assign responsibility for supervision and mentoring, so interns feel they are being taken care of.
- Let staff members know when an intern is coming on board and the role he or she will be playing so there are no surprises and people can offer a helping hand. In addition, hold your current team accountable for the experience of the intern.

When you screen a pool of qualified candidates, you should interview them the same way you would a full-time employee. Candidates may also be open to longer-term internships or part-time employment, which can help reduce any concerns you may have about continuity and the need to continually train new interns.

Work with Millennials

Millennials are coming of age and are projected to make up 50% of the workforce by 2020.* Employers need to understand that the work habits, communications style, and expectations of this group will be different from those of baby boomers. Setting expectations appropriately, and providing a collaborative, team-oriented environment with regular feedback and coaching will help keep these employees satisfied.

Consider:

- Adjusting job descriptions to appeal to millennials by using terms such as teamwork, collaboration, mentorship, education, and training
- Discussing potential career paths up front, and what it takes to go from one position to another
- Having them speak with other millennials who have moved up the ladder
- Hiring millennials as interns so they can experience the environment firsthand
- Providing job flexibility so they can balance work with outside activities
- Offering regular feedback that focuses on the positives and provides clear suggestions on how to hone different skills
- Being inclusive and asking for their opinions and ideas
- Keeping them challenged and learning new things

*"Three Reasons You Need to Adopt a Millennial Mindset Regardless of Your Age," *Forbes,* October 2012, http://www.forbes.com/sites/jeannemeister/2012/10/05/millennialmindse/.

Have a Great Employee Story

While most firms understand the importance of having a compelling story for clients, fewer can clearly articulate a similar story for staff members. Yet according to the Corporate Leadership Council,* a strong employee story can enable organizations to reach 50% deeper into the labor market to attract passive candidates, improve commitment of employees by up to 37%, and reduce new-hire compensation premiums by up to 50%. Given the potential impact a well-crafted employee story can have on your firm, you should consider taking steps to both create and communicate it.

Employees typically care about tangible items, such as compensation and benefits, as well as intangible items, such as the opportunity to collaborate with innovative people, further develop their skills, or balance job and life activities. Your story should capture the things you know your people value, as well as the unique aspects of your culture that aren't easy for a competitor to duplicate.

When looking to attract millennials, Dr. Chaffin says you need to keep in mind that young people today want to believe in their firm's mission and feel they are serving a useful cause that's helping to make a difference in people's lives. This provides the opportunity to discuss how an advisor helps people when they are going through life transitions, whether it's a marriage, the birth of a child, or the loss of a job.

When thinking about what to emphasize in your employee story, consider whether you:

- Offer noncompensation rewards that set you apart.
- Provide unique training and mentoring opportunities.
- Emphasize respect for clients, business partners, and employees in all that you do.
- Provide a fun and flexible work environment.
- Have strong teamwork that distinguishes you.
- Let employees affect the client experience and success of the business.

Pick the three or four things that rise to the top of the list that are strong points for your firm and pull them together in a paragraph.

*"Rebuilding the Employment Value Proposition: Four Strategies to Improve Employee Effort and Retention," Corporate Leadership Council, The Corporate Executive Board Company, 2010. More than 50 organizations participated in the Council's Employee Value Proposition Survey from Q4 2008 to Q2 2009, representing the global workforce.

A Hypothetical Example: ABCD Advisory

ABCD Advisory was introduced in Chapter 4 on client engagement. The firm was founded in 1987 by two former Peace Corps volunteers who wanted to start an RIA with a focus on encouraging positive social change. The team deals exclusively with family office solutions, particularly multigenerational solutions, and they chose to capture the following points in their employee story:

- **Ownership in the firm,** because it pushes excellence, creates a common set of interests, and provides an incentive to build the business for the future
- **A team approach centered on the client,** because it creates a collegial atmosphere where collaboration can help spawn new, creative ideas to better serve clients
- **A disciplined environment,** because it provides clarity and keeps the business on track
- **A sense of caring for others,** because it's personally rewarding to think we are giving to the community as we work

For illustrative purposes only.

They summarized these points in the following way in their employee story:

We are a tight-knit, disciplined organization where employees are focused on serving our clients well and growing a business we all have a stake in. We work in a highly collaborative fashion and value and reward productive teamwork. We show the highest respect for our business partners and coworkers, and are actively involved in philanthropic endeavors to improve the lives of others.

This hypothetical employee story may appeal to some people and not to others, helping to identify candidates who are well suited to the firm and its mission.

Go to begreater.com to access additional resources supporting Chapter 5.

Develop Employees through Personal Growth Plans and Regular Feedback

Talented people are looking for a career — not just a job. They want to learn skills, gain experience, and be in a position to take on additional responsibilities over time. By mentoring them and spending time on development plans and regular performance reviews, you can demonstrate that you truly care about their success and want to help guide them along the way.

Learn About

- Mentoring staff
- Customizing development plans
- Conducting regular performance reviews

The stories that follow discuss the importance of mentoring individuals and having consistent and thorough development plans to help take the skills and behaviors of your best and brightest to the next level. This is as important for smaller firms as it is for larger ones.

"This business is all about people — they define our success. We take very seriously our responsibility to help them develop their skills, be fulfilled in their careers, and provide for their families."

RICHARD BURRIDGE, FOUNDING PARTNER, CEO, AND CHIEF INVESTMENT OFFICER
RMB CAPITAL

CREATE AN ENVIRONMENT FOR SUCCESS

Richard Burridge says RMB Capital is looking for long-term, career-oriented individuals and has created an environment that enables them to grow and meet their goals.

SAYS BURRIDGE:

Our wealth management business is organized into teams that include different levels of wealth advisors and client associates—all of whom are looking to advance to the next level and, ultimately, run their own team.

> "To succeed, every employee needs somebody who is in their corner and investing time in the training and development process." RICHARD BURRIDGE

We have a clearly defined career path that outlines the minimum requirements for advancement every step of the way—from entry level to senior wealth manager. It includes the typical length of time in each position and what needs to be accomplished in order to move forward; the entire path would generally take at least ten years to go through. Of course, we have also laid out compensation ranges for each level. This is more formalized today than it was in the past, but it's essentially the same system we have been successfully using since we started the firm. It helps set expectations all around.

There are a number of things I think are important for employees to thrive. First of all, they need to have a strong mentor. In our wealth management business, each team's senior wealth manager is ultimately responsible for training, developing, and mentoring—directly or indirectly—all the people on his or her team.

I also think it's important to give people tasks where they are likely to succeed. For example, we don't ask our younger people to develop new business, which is typically difficult for someone just starting out because they simply don't have the expertise, the confidence, or the personal network to be effective. We assign responsibilities that are consistent with each employee's level of experience and that will provide a sense of accomplishment. We also aim to balance those tasks with bigger challenges that will give employees opportunities to grow.

Last, but not least, employees need regular performance reviews to openly discuss their progress, areas of strength, and areas for improvement. I believe people will only realize their full potential if we invest in them, support them, and provide constructive feedback—and if they take ownership for their growth as well.

We really strive to be a place where employees can envision spending their entire career. So we focus on hiring people who fit with our values and culture, who are genuinely motivated to continue improving, and who will do their part to help their fellow employees do the same.

When we find great people, we create opportunities for them. For example, we have an employee who started his career with us right out of college, has been promoted a number of times, and is four or five years away from running a wealth management team. He and his new wife are originally from Washington, DC, and wanted to move back at some point to be closer to family. So, we decided to open an office there and build around him. After all, he's a highly valued employee who has been totally dedicated to our firm and does a phenomenal job with clients. This will support our expansion strategy and mitigates concerns about fostering our culture in a new office or having to closely oversee the operation.

Key Insight

People are your most valuable asset and you need to take the time to describe an appropriate career path for each individual, and coach them along the way. Give your management specific responsibilities for mentoring and training staff so you can reap the benefits of a skilled team.

CUSTOMIZE DEVELOPMENT PLANS

Adam Birenbaum says the leadership at Buckingham Asset Management feels one of the greatest challenges in the industry is finding top talent. The firm uses customized development programs to help attract advisors who value this personalized approach.

SAYS BIRENBAUM:

I think one of the biggest challenges this industry faces is finding next-generation talent—those individuals who can service clients in the same way our predecessors did. We actually look for younger associates across many different professions, including CPAs, lawyers, and educators. If people enjoy sharing information and solving client problems, we feel we can turn them into great wealth advisors.

"Find good people, give them great opportunities, and fabulous things will happen." ADAM BIRENBAUM

Attracting and developing top talent is a key strategic initiative for us. We pay a lot of attention to nurturing our associates, and do this through ongoing mentorship, continuous feedback, and meaningful career advancement. I also think that a firm that's striving to be greater needs to commit to a person's customized growth plan and help them be as successful as they want to be. The key word is customized. Everybody learns and grows differently, so you need to cater to the individual. This is something younger team members in particular really value—a demonstrated commitment to their personal development. They want to feel they are being challenged and learning new skills, so you need to discuss their specific situation and craft a plan that will expand their capabilities and let them have different experiences.

Key Insight

You may find excellent associates outside the financial services industry. Because everyone learns somewhat differently, customized development plans can reflect a person's unique skills and behaviors to help them meet their career objectives. This is especially important for younger associates who may place a higher value on a personalized approach to coaching and mentoring.

CONDUCT REGULAR PERFORMANCE REVIEWS

Russ Hill says Halbert Hargrove Global Advisors follows a very systematic approach to setting goals for employees and monitoring their performance. This includes tying goals to the firm's strategic initiatives and conducting quarterly reviews to evaluate progress.

SAYS HILL:

Our biggest asset is our people, and everyone has a separate development plan. It starts with outlining the core job and what the person needs to do to excel in that role. It's then modified depending on additional tasks they may have because he or she is assigned to one team or another.

"Everyone in our firm has a personal development plan and a formal quarterly review with our president and COO. This isn't lip service—we follow the program very seriously." RUSS HILL

Regular reviews include an evaluation of how well people are meeting their objectives and where they may need help. The review also includes an assessment of their ability to delegate, as we feel you can't progress if you do everything on your own. Because good teamwork is essential to us, too, we also look at instances where an individual has helped someone else in the firm do their job better. Interestingly, our highest-performing people are the ones who value these discussions the most, as they constantly want to know how they can further hone their skills.

Depending on the particular position, monitoring and feedback may be tied to our strategic planning process. For example, our middle managers have a large portion of their review tied to our annual strategic initiatives, because they have responsibility for seeing things through.

Key Insight

Giving regular feedback to employees is essential for them to gauge whether they are meeting your expectations, and to define appropriate development plans. Put in place a schedule for reviews and have managers be well prepared to provide constructive comments on performance.

[5.2]

CONNECTING THE DOTS

CREATE DEVELOPMENT PLANS

Mentorship, feedback, career development, and the "softer" elements of job satisfaction should be priorities for firms of all sizes. Clear performance expectations and development plans can help you and your employees get on the same page and avoid any frustrations that may arise from not knowing what's expected for success.

To help create development plans that staff members can follow, consider starting with "performance inventories" that list the capabilities you are looking for in a specific position. For example, a financial planning professional might be expected to be analytical, familiar with financial planning software, capable of making sound recommendations, and adept at interacting with clients. With this clearly described, you can have a productive dialogue regarding a person's strengths and challenges as they relate to these capabilities.

Performance inventories let employees perform a self-evaluation, which helps keep them actively involved in the process. For each capability, they should rate whether they feel they are exceeding expectations, meeting expectations, or need to improve. They can then meet with their manager to compare notes, get feedback, and discuss goals for the development plan.

When an employee and his or her manager completes the performance inventory throughout the year, they can jointly discuss how well the person is doing relative to his or her development plan. Informal feedback on a regular basis can also be a great motivator. Simply recognizing good work when you see it, or providing constructive suggestions to help someone perform better or learn new skills, can go a long way.

CONDUCT FORMAL PERFORMANCE REVIEWS

Discussions about performance inventories and the development plan can reduce the likelihood of having any surprises during the performance review, and feed into a more formal, written review. While performance is naturally tied to compensation, the message about performance can often get lost when people are thinking about their salary level. Given this, you might consider decoupling performance and compensation discussions.

In some cases, your assessment of an employee's performance may not align with his or her view. If this happens, explain the process that was followed to collect data and feedback and then ask the employee to explain why he or she disagrees. Make it clear that you have an open mind, especially if the person can provide examples that would change your perspective. Offer to schedule another meeting within a few days to allow the person to consider your feedback and do some research.

Sometimes, you may just have to agree to disagree. In either case, you should have the employee provide a signed copy of the written review for your personnel records. Should there come a time when you need to discipline an employee, it may be helpful to show that the performance feedback was received by the employee.

If you are a leader at the firm, you should also do a self-assessment and grade yourself on the strength of your firm's mission and strategy. In addition, ask how well you are doing when it comes to communicating with staff and motivating them to meet the firm's objectives. You may even decide to gather employee feedback to gain additional insight into your own areas for improvement.

Go to begreater.com to access additional resources supporting Chapter 5.

Engage Employees by Providing Both Financial and Nonfinancial Rewards

Learn About

- Being inclusive
- Recognition and rewards
- The role of compensation
- Instilling confidence

According to the Corporate Leadership Council's study mentioned earlier in the chapter, there are five factors that drive performance and retention:*

- **Rewards:** compensation, benefits
- **Opportunity:** development, organizational growth
- **Organization:** client prestige, respect, empowerment, well-known brand
- **Work:** alignment with job interests, innovation, recognition, work-life balance
- **People:** camaraderie, collegial environment, quality coworkers

The firms we interviewed look at a broad set of factors as well, and say engaged employees enjoy coming to work, are motivated by what they do, and show enthusiasm for their success and the success of others. In short, they are emotionally connected to the firm and are typically willing to go beyond the call of duty to meet—or exceed—the expectations of management and their peers. Naturally, engaged employees are also far less likely to leave for what they perceive to be a better opportunity. In the pages that follow, five RIAs describe steps they have taken to connect with their employees, show they care about their professional and personal lives, and promote overall job satisfaction.

> "A smart human capital strategy is key to a successful wealth management company." MICHAEL NATHANSON, CHAIRMAN, CEO, AND PRESIDENT THE COLONY GROUP

*Examples only. Each factor has a number of other components.

GIVE TO GET

While compensation is an important motivator for employees at Halbert Hargrove Global Advisors, Russ Hill believes it's equally important to provide challenging assignments, recognize successes, and show you truly care about people.

SAYS HILL:

> "People get engaged when they have meaningful jobs, have the authority to execute, and are paid fairly." RUSS HILL

Over the past few years, we have tried various compensation schemes. While you need to have a competitive salary, I think job satisfaction and engagement are rarely just about money. If you give people important work, pay them fairly, and provide a degree of autonomy, then they are happy. We involve our staff in all aspects of the business, including our annual strategic planning process and ongoing review of the company's performance.

You also need to show employees that you care about them, and we provide support in many different ways. This includes a profit-sharing plan and employee benefits. We also have a "fun bonus," which everyone enjoys. Whenever we have a new client relationship moving along, for example, we may provide on-the-spot rewards. It isn't a lot of money, but each member of the team that brought in the business gets something.

We also have an equity plan whereby we determine who can buy into the company and then finance it. This can be a significant bump in value over time for people who are moving up in the management structure, and having skin in the game can be a really strong motivator.

We provide support in many other forms as well. We pay for our staff to get executive education and various certifications, we have a housing bonus for employees who move within twenty miles of the office, and we match contributions to 529 plans and daycare services. We even decided to build a nursery in the office so new moms could come to work with their babies.

Many people look at what we do and wonder why we spend so much money. My response is that our employees are engaged and give back as a result. For example, a number of years ago, I decided that everyone could leave at two o'clock in the afternoon on Fridays in the summer. Without asking, people started coming in at six in the morning so they could get their work done. They are very committed to the business.

Key Insight

Employees who are treated well and rewarded for their efforts will take pride in the firm and be willing to work hard to see it be successful. Consider unique ways to recognize them for their contributions and accomplishments.

BUILD ENGAGEMENT IN MULTIPLE WAYS

Blaine Lourd says an attractive compensation package is an important part of LourdMurray's employee value proposition — but it isn't the only thing that counts. Challenging jobs, support for education, and a productive work environment all combine to strengthen employee commitment to the firm.

SAYS LOURD:

You can use compensation to get people engaged, but that's just part of the story. We also want to have an educated and forward-thinking organization, and will pay for people to take courses and obtain credentials. We have three people studying for the Certified Financial Planner® certification at the moment, and we'll even consider paying if someone wants to do an MBA.

> "When people are compensated well, are in an organization that's growing, and are having fun, they are very motivated and do good work." BLAINE LOURD

We send all our administrative staff to a local university for basic finance courses, and there are many occasions for other members of our team to attend seminars and training sessions through our third-party business partners. These cover a variety of topics, ranging from how to use specific technology applications to hot issues in compliance to building leadership talent. This also enables our staff to network and see how other people are approaching the business.

I think office aesthetics and interactions help to engage employees as well. We have made a point of having a beautiful and productive work environment, and have redone the cubicles so they are more ergonomic. We also organize a lot of team outings that include baseball and basketball games that bring everyone together in a social setting. In addition, we pay for breakfast every Monday, fill the refrigerators with all sorts of goodies, and regularly order in pizza.

The best way to engage people, however, is to give them a challenging job, and help them own that job. People get empowered when you give them the leeway to do things their way and don't micromanage everything. It helps their ambition come through.

I also think you have to lead from a positive standpoint at all times. Of course, you have to discipline people now and again, but mostly you have to positively motivate them, and make sure they are challenged and enjoy what they do.

Key Insight

There is a range of tangible and intangible factors that will affect employee morale, so you need to understand what people really value and offer a number of motivators. The tone of the leadership team can also have a strong impact on the morale and attitudes of team members, so every manager should try to remain upbeat even during stressful situations.

DEMONSTRATE YOUR VALUE

Rick Buoncore says the staff at MAI Wealth Advisors had gone through a number of owners in a short period of time, which made them question what the latest round of management could offer. As the new owner, he needed to demonstrate that he could turn things around to get employees on board with his game plan.

SAYS BUONCORE:

My team had been through a lot because the firm had been sold several times before, and they were very skeptical of any ideas I had, given their past experiences. I decided I had to show them firsthand that I had a good plan of action. I paid myself the same as they were making, and I worked hard to bring in new business.

"I bought a firm that had great people with great talent, but they were exhausted by the previous series of sales they had gone through. I needed to get them engaged." RICK BUONCORE

Initially, they had a lot of questions about what I was doing and why I was spending money on things like marketing but, as we grew, they got it. Now everyone is on board, which proves you can engage people if you pull your weight and show that your ideas can have a significant impact on the bottom line.

Key Insight

At times, you may have a team that's skeptical about the viability of your plans. Becoming actively involved as a leader, and showing that your plans are sound and can positively impact the business, can help bring people on board.

STREAMLINE AREAS OF RESPONSIBILITY

Michael Nathanson says The Colony Group has grown to such a size that the firm now has professional management. This specialization of labor has created efficiencies, while improving job satisfaction.

SAYS NATHANSON:

When we were a smaller firm, everyone on staff was dealing with a range of activities, including clients, portfolio management, operations, vendor management, compliance, and more. Over the years, our growth has enabled us to go in the extreme opposite direction. We have evolved to the point where we now have professional management, which includes full-time chief executive, operations, compliance, and business development officers, plus a controller and others. We have gone from everyone wearing multiple hats to everyone wearing one hat.

"Times have really changed since we were first founded, when people had to wear multiple hats." MICHAEL NATHANSON

Of course, part of our growth has been fueled by merger and acquisition activity. Combining with other like-minded advisors has helped us acquire new talent and refocus existing personnel on more specific functions. We think this specialization of labor has made us more efficient and effective in serving our clients. We also think it has helped with job satisfaction, because there are full-time, fully dedicated resources our staff can rely on. This helps us be very clear about who is accountable for what, which makes it more likely tasks will be attended to and much easier for me to run the firm.

Key Insight

As your firm begins to grow, you may have an opportunity to create more positions that are fully dedicated to a particular role, like operations or technology. This specialization can increase efficiencies as well as job satisfaction when people aren't being pulled in multiple directions.

CREATE A THRIVING STAFF

Marty Bicknell of Mariner Holdings has taken a number of steps to help the firm's associates focus on the things they do best. He is also taking steps to help younger people learn more about the advisory industry and the types of careers that are available.

SAYS BICKNELL:

As our firm has grown, we have made a number of significant changes, including separating business development from advice. When you look at the wirehouse model, typically the best business development person isn't the best advice-giver. Given the usual compensation models that exist, that means these good advisors aren't making much money. We want to attract the best advice-givers and compensate them for retention — and retention only. We can then let the skilled business development professionals bring on new relationships, without having much client responsibility. Splitting these two roles has worked extremely well for us.

> "When we started the firm in 2006, we had eight associates; today, we have four hundred and seventy-five. That's given us the opportunity to do things differently." MARTY BICKNELL

One of the other changes we made very early on was to separate wealth advice from investment advice, because we want our advisors focused on helping clients achieve their goals, not spending time trying to pick the best stock. So we support our advisors with a fully dedicated investment team that does all the research and helps them with the investment process. We surround our advisors with other experts too, like people who are very knowledgeable about taxes, estate planning, and insurance.

We also hear a lot about the aging advisor and the need to add younger people to our ranks. To increase the flow of new talent into the profession, I think members of our industry need to work together to adjust any misconceptions that may be out there about the business given negative comments in the media. We need to educate the next generation about what we do so they understand this can be a noble profession that helps people. To support this, we are going to endow four chairs at local universities for the Mariner School of Financial Planning. We are partnering with a group that will help us develop the curriculum so we can raise awareness about RIAs and train students on becoming a fiduciary.

Key Insight

Firms need to create job responsibilities that enable their current employees to excel. At the same time, they need to be spokespeople for the profession to attract new advisors who are dedicated to helping people address many important financial and life transition decisions.

[5.3]

CONNECTING THE DOTS

ENGAGE EMPLOYEES

The RIA stories provide a number of interesting takeaways to consider as you look at ways to strengthen the connection you have with your employees — and that they have with your firm. For example:

- **Be inclusive.** Involve employees in strategic issues so they are in tune with the firm's overall goals and the role they can play in making things happen.
- **Show you care about each individual.** Demonstrate a genuine interest in employees and their needs and desires, touch base regularly to see how they are doing, and customize their development plans and performance reviews to capture how they can use their unique attributes and skills to support the firm's mission.
- **Present challenges.** Provide meaningful work to keep interest levels high and empower your employees to take action to get things done. Of course, provide opportunities for advancement so they don't feel they are stagnating at any point.
- **Recognize and reward.** Acknowledge a job well done that supports your firm's vision and values, and consider surprise awards as a fun and cost-effective way to show appreciation.
- **Think beyond compensation.** Invest in professional development and consider providing other benefits and perks to make people feel valued.
- **Be fair.** Treat everyone with the same dignity and respect, and research industry compensation levels so you know you are in line with market rates.
- **Communicate extensively.** Let people know what's going on with the firm and create an environment of trust where they feel they can weigh in and express their views without any negative ramifications.

Go to begreater.com to access additional resources supporting Chapter 5.

In a service industry, people are a firm's foundation. Happy and highly motivated individuals can make the difference when it comes to the client experience, the employee experience, and the overall success of the business. It's essential to spend the time to build and maintain a collaborative and rewarding work environment to help you attract and retain top talent that can keep your firm moving forward. Don't underestimate the fact that this environment is shaped in part by leadership and how well senior management is doing its job. This includes the creation and execution of a meaningful longer-term strategy, regular outreach, and clear communication about how the firm is doing and where it's headed.

We have now touched on five areas: business models, planning, technology, client engagement, and teams. In the summary that follows, we take another look at how these areas work together, and the importance of addressing each and every one of them if you are to supercharge your business.

[Conclusion]

A Few Final Thoughts

"The rung of a ladder was neve meant to rest upon, but only t hold a man's foot long enoug to enable him to put the othe somewhat higher." THOMAS HENRY HUXLEY

As we indicated at the beginning of this book, many advisors have told us that today's environment requires that RIAs continually try to reach higher. Too many changes are taking place to be complacent. Firms need to think strategically on a number of fronts if they are to create a strong and sustainable business. Our aim in writing this book has been to underscore this fact and to provide insights about how different RIAs are taking steps to position themselves as a preferred advisory firm for investors, associates, and other teams. We hope the stories, practical considerations, and supporting resources have provided takeaways that you can apply to your own situation. Here are the five lessons we shared.

From Chapter 1: You can't stand still. You need to continually evaluate your business model and see what new opportunities are available. There are now many different ways to operate an RIA, which is affecting the choices that are being made by firms new to the space, as well as by firms that have been in business for a long time. Infrastructure and support services are more readily available to help put a firm on a higher trajectory, and more sources of capital can be accessed to launch new services, expand locations, and bring on other advisory teams.

What does this imply for the future? Will we see an influx of RIAs given the support that's available to help launch firms, increased consolidation as the number of M&A transactions increases, and expanded and diversified lines of business in response to emerging opportunities? Only time will tell. What's clear is that change is in the air and you need to stay on top of market dynamics to assess the implications for your firm — now and in the future. As Marty Bicknell said, with all that's going on, you have to continually evaluate and evolve your business to stay cutting edge.

From Chapter 2: You need to have a disciplined approach to planning. This is no longer simply an option if you are going to focus on the initiatives that are most critical for your firm's long-term success.

While it may be possible to have an RIA that runs smoothly and serves its clients well without having a well-articulated plan, it's hard to imagine being truly successful if you don't have a clear vision of where you are headed, how you are going to get there, and who is going to make it happen. Firms need a strategic plan to stay on top of a handful of priority initiatives, as well as a succession plan to map out the eventual transition of responsibilities and ownership to new leadership.

Looking forward, we believe planning will become even more essential for RIAs. There is simply too much happening not to lay out a roadmap for the future. Digital advice, Gen X/Y clients and employees, and a growing base of female investors are just a few of the developments that are changing the landscape. Evaluating different scenarios can help prepare you for a range of possible outcomes and keep you on track to advance the business. As Greg Erwin said, what you gain from planning can be fantastic if you are committed to it.

From Chapter 3: Technology isn't just about efficiency and productivity today. New developments are helping to redefine the client experience and serve as competitive differentiators.

Technology has always been a large component of advisory firms, and many infrastructure improvements have been made possible of late, driven by more powerful offerings and better integration among systems. But the big news is that technology has moved from being an operational issue to being a business development and client retention issue. Advisors are seizing opportunities to leverage applications to improve how they service, communicate, and collaborate with the investor community.

As we consider where this is all headed, Fidelity's "office of the future" gave us a glimpse of what things could look like in a few years, showcasing collaborative workspaces, wearable devices, and more. This seems like a natural progression given the importance of technology for the next generation of clients. As Russ Hill said, younger clients and employees alike want to access information where and how it suits them. We see the demand for 24/7, tech-savvy advisors only increasing over time.

From Chapter 4: You need to up your game when it comes to marketing and business development. RIAs are honing their skills on this front and taking steps to stand out in a crowded marketplace. Marketing and business development have often been weak spots for many RIAs, but times are changing. Firms are evaluating the type of client who is best suited to their business and sharpening their message. They are also pursuing new outreach strategies and adding social media, direct mail, and other techniques to the mix to leverage resources and reach a broader audience.

We believe RIAs will continue to hone their skills when it comes to client acquisition and retention strategies. This will include the refinement of the early-stage initiatives we see under way today to connect with tomorrow's wealthy. We believe women, younger investors, and next-generation family members of current clients will begin to take center stage. Firms will spend more time trying to understand what appeals to these groups and how they should position their offerings to attract new business. As Jane Williams said, concentrating on specific types of investors can help set you up for success.

 **From Chapter 5: Acquisition and retention strategies are just as important to building a strong team as they are to building a strong client base.**

People are a firm's most valuable asset, so you need to make smart hires and take steps to adequately develop, challenge, and motivate all staff members. It's also important to keep in mind that potential new hires will likely be most interested in firms that can lay out a career path with growth opportunities, see development as a priority, and offer a range of attractive benefits.

We see the concept of talent management gaining much more attention in the future as older advisors begin retiring and competition intensifies for the best and brightest people to fill their shoes. As firms think about staffing, we believe they'll carefully consider the diversity that exists among their professionals, and pay greater attention to the needs of millennials who value collaboration, a good work-life balance, and being challenged. As Michael Nathanson said, a smart human capital strategy is key to a successful wealth management company.

MOVING FORWARD

In a world where good enough is no longer an option, it's essential to continually strive to be greater on many fronts. Looking through the lens of the points of view we have developed, we have touched on five areas we believe need to be handled extremely well to create a strong advisory firm. While each area is important in and of itself, what's most important is that the five areas work together for maximum impact. Clients and employees alike want to be associated with RIAs that have a sound business model, know where they are headed, are tech savvy, and address the issues they feel are important.

We hope you have been inspired by reading this wisdom from the front lines and that the insights we have shared—combined with practical dos and don'ts—can help you move the dial to make your financial advisory firm Be Greater℠.

Firm Profiles

We would like to express our sincere gratitude to the clients of Fidelity Institutional Wealth Services featured in this book, who took the time to share their stories with us. These firms, large and small, are striving to be greater, and we appreciate hearing about the different action plans they have in place to further build their business.

Please note that all AUM/AUA* figures mentioned herein are as of March 31, 2014, unless otherwise noted, and all employee numbers are as of the summer of 2014.

AdvicePeriod, LLC

Corporate Headquarters	**Los Angeles, California**
Person Interviewed	**Steve Lockshin, Founder and Principal, AdvicePeriod; Chairman, Convergent Wealth Advisors**
Date Firm Founded	**Launched 2014**
Approximate AUM/AUA	**$100 million AUM; $1 billion AUA**
Approximate Number of Employees	**6**

*Assets under advisement.

BakerAvenue

Corporate Headquarters	**San Francisco, California**
Other Locations	**Irving, Texas; New York, New York; Palm Beach Gardens, Florida**
Persons Interviewed	**Jerry Luff, Chief Operating Officer**
	Doug Couden, Chief Investment Officer
Date Firm Founded	**2004**
Approximate AUM	**$1.1 billion**
Approximate Number of Employees	**22**

Banyan Partners, LLC

Corporate Headquarters	**Palm Beach Gardens, Florida**
Other Locations	**Atlanta, Georgia; Boston, Massachusetts; Coral Gables, Florida; Naples, Florida; Madison, Wisconsin; New York, New York; Plano, Texas; San Francisco, California**
Persons Interviewed	**Peter Raimondi, Founder and CEO**
	Sherri Daniels, Chief Operating Officer
Date Firm Founded	**2006**
Approximate AUM/AUA	**$3.6 billion AUM; $900 million AUA**
Approximate Number of Employees	**87**

Brinton Eaton Wealth Advisors, a Mariner Wealth Advisors Firm

Corporate Headquarters	**Madison, New Jersey**
Other Location	**New York, New York**
Person Interviewed	**Bob DiQuollo, CEO and Principal**
Date Firm Founded	**1988**
Date Joined Mariner	**2012**
Approximate AUM	**$800 million**
Approximate Number of Employees	**19**

Buckingham Asset Management, LLC, and BAM Advisor Services LLC, a Focus Financial Partner

Corporate Headquarters	**St. Louis, Missouri**
Other Locations	**Burlington, Iowa; Cupertino, California; Dallas, Texas; Irvine, California; Santa Rosa, California**
Person Interviewed	**Adam Birenbaum, CEO**
Date Firm Founded	**Buckingham: 1994**
	BAM: 1997
Date Joined Focus	**2007**
Approximate AUM/AUA	**Buckingham: $6.5 billion**
	BAM: $17 billion
Approximate Number of Employees	**170**

The Colony Group, LLC, a Focus Financial Partner

Corporate Headquarters	**Boston, Massachusetts**
Other Locations	**Armonk, New York; Naples, Florida; New York, New York**
Persons Interviewed	**Michael Nathanson, Chairman, CEO, and President**
	Bob Glovsky, Vice Chair and Senior Financial Counselor
Date Firm Founded	**1986**
Date Joined Focus	**2011**
Approximate AUM	**$3.5 billion**
Approximate Number of Employees	**68**

Halbert Hargrove Global Advisors, LLC

Corporate Headquarters	**Long Beach, California**
Other Locations	**Bellevue, Washington; Denver, Colorado; Houston, Texas; San Diego, California; Scottsdale, Arizona**
	Halbert Hargrove and Altaira: London, United Kingdom; Geneva, Switzerland
Person Interviewed	**Russ Hill, Chairman and CEO**
Date Firm Founded	**1998**
Approximate AUM	**$4 billion**
Approximate Number of Employees	**40**

HSW Advisors, HighTower

Corporate Headquarters	**HighTower: Chicago, Illinois**
	HSW Advisors: New York, New York
Other Locations	**HighTower has 48 teams in 38 locations across the country**
Person Interviewed	**Jordan Waxman, Managing Director, Partner**
Date Firm Founded	**HighTower: 2008**
	HSW Advisors: 1996
Date Joined HighTower	**2012**
Approximate AUM	**HSW Advisors: $1.3 billion**
Approximate Number of Employees	**9**

Keatley Wealth Management, LLC

Corporate Headquarters	**Charlotte, North Carolina**
Person Interviewed	**Karen Keatley, President and Chief Investment Officer**
Date Firm Founded	**2003**
Approximate AUM	**$45 million**
Approximate Number of Employees	**3**

LourdMurray

Corporate Headquarters	**Beverly Hills, California**
Other Location	**New Orleans, Louisiana**
Person Interviewed	**Blaine Lourd, Managing Member**
Date Firm Founded	**2006**
Approximate AUM	**$3 billion**
Approximate Number of Employees	**23**

MAI Wealth Advisors, LLC

Corporate Headquarters	**Cleveland, Ohio**
Other Locations	**Boston, Massachusetts; Jacksonville, Florida**
Person Interviewed	**Rick Buoncore, Managing Partner**
Date Firm Founded	**1973**
Approximate AUM*	**$3.9 billion**
Approximate Number of Employees	**82**

*As of June 30, 2014.

Mariner Holdings:* Mariner Wealth Advisors, LLC, and FirstPoint Financial, LLC

Corporate Headquarters	**Leawood, Kansas**
Other Locations	**California, Nebraska, New Jersey, New York, Ohio, Oklahoma**
Person Interviewed	**Marty Bicknell, CEO**
Date Firm Founded	**Mariner Holdings: 2006**
	Mariner Wealth Advisors: 2006
	FirstPoint Financial: 2013
Approximate AUM	**Mariner Holdings: $35 billion**
	Mariner Wealth Advisors: $9 billion
	FirstPoint Financial: $115 million
Approximate Number of Employees	**Mariner Holdings: 392**
	Mariner Wealth Advisors: 186
	FirstPoint Financial: 15

*Mariner Holdings also includes Montage Investments, not discussed in this book.

Pactolus Private Wealth Management LLC

Corporate Headquarters	**McLean, Virginia**
Person Interviewed	**Alan Harter, Managing Director**
Date Firm Founded	**2011**
Approximate AUM	**$400 million**
Approximate Number of Employees	**10**

RMB Capital: RMB Wealth Management, RMB Asset Management, RMB Retirement Plan Solutions, and Iron Road Capital Partners

Corporate Headquarters	**Chicago, Illinois**
Other Locations	**Denver, Colorado; Jackson Hole, Wyoming**
Persons Interviewed	**Richard Burridge, Founding Partner, CEO, and Chief Investment Officer**
	Walt Melcher, V.P. and Director of RMB Retirement Plan Solutions
Date Firm Founded	**2005**
Approximate AUM	**$3.8 billion**
Approximate Number of Employees	**100**

Rockwood Wealth Management, LLC

Corporate Headquarters	**New Hope, Pennsylvania**
Other Location	**Annapolis, Maryland**
Person Interviewed	**John Augenblick, President**
Date Firm Founded	**2009**
Approximate AUM	**$260 million**
Approximate Number of Employees	**8**

Sand Hill Global Advisors, LLC

Corporate Headquarters	**Palo Alto, California**
Persons Interviewed	**Jane Williams, Chair and Co-Founder**
	Brian Dombkowski, CEO and Chief Investment Officer
Date Firm Founded	**1982**
Approximate AUM	**$1.3 billion**
Approximate Number of Employees	**21**

Sapient Private Wealth Management Services, LLC, a Focus Financial Partner

Corporate Headquarters	**Eugene, Oregon**
Person Interviewed	**Greg Erwin, Co-Founder and Partner**
Date Firm Founded	**Formed and joined Focus: 2010**
Approximate AUM	**$700 million**
Approximate Number of Employees	**11**

United Capital Financial Advisers, LLC

Corporate Headquarters	**United Capital: Newport Beach, California** **Trevethan's team: San Francisco, California**
Other Locations	**50+ locations across the country**
Person Interviewed	**Kelly Trevethan, Regional Managing Director**
Date Firm Founded	**United Capital: 2004**
Date Team Joined	**2008**
Approximate AUM	**United Capital: $10 billion** **Trevethan's team: $445 million**
Approximate Number of Employees	**United Capital: 400** **Trevethan's team: 10**

Waldron Wealth Management

Corporate Headquarters	**Bridgeville, Pennsylvania**
Person Interviewed	**John Waldron, Founder and CEO**
Date Firm Founded	**1995**
Date Became an RIA	**2012**
Approximate AUM*	**$1.1 billion**
Approximate Number of Employees	**26**

*As of June 30, 2014.